Seeds of Transformation

Seeds of Transformation

A 52-Step Journey
To Enlightenment

MAGGIE EROTOKRITOU

This edition edited by Magaer Lennox

Cover design by Damian Keenan

Text design by The Bridgewater Book Company

Printed and bound by WS Bookwell, Finland

1 2 3 4 5 6 7 8 9 10 11 12 13 12 11 10 09 08 07

Published by

Findhorn Press

305a The Park, Findhorn

Forres IV36 3TE

Scotland, UK

Telephone +44-(0)1309-690582

Fax +44-(0)1309-690036

info@findhornpress.com

www.findhornpress.com

To the I AM Presence,
and to the Cosmic Beings that guide our journey
towards enlightenment

Contents

An Introduction to the Seeds

The Seeds of Transformation are amazing, practical tools of self growth that will enable you to transform your consciousness and thereby change the way you live your life and see the world. They will empower you to attract that which you desire and deserve and teach you how to interact with life in a new way. Through working with the Seeds, you will learn how to cut through illusions and to see life differently through crystal clear lenses.

Each Seed is like a mantra that is placed in your consciousness and reveals and unfolds that which you need to know so that transformation can take place. Each Seed continues working even after you have let it go and moved onto the next one. The Seeds have been given in a specific order and as such they should be worked with in this order. There are energetic threads that link each Seed to the next and together they create a synthesis within the brain.

It is recommended that you work with each individual Seed for a whole week and to keep it in your mind as much as possible throughout the day. Every sentence describing the Seeds contains multiple Seedlings, ideas, and new thought forms to be contemplated upon. Hence the Seeds can be worked with again and again over a period of many years, for you will always discover something new that you had not acknowledged or noticed before. The more your consciousness expands, the more the Seeds will reveal themselves to you.

The Seeds are an initiation into new realms of consciousness that bring clarity, wisdom, and depth to a degree you may never have encountered before. The Seeds offer many opportunities and openings that will greatly enhance your life. They are a birthing process, which will carry you forward; each one will nourish and help you to grow, expand, and discover more.

The Seeds help you to become more conscious of what you are thinking and doing, and show you where your strengths and weaknesses lie. Planting the Seeds of Transformation in your consciousness on a daily basis will create transformation on every level of your life.

The Seeds were given to me in meditation so that they could be shared as a personal tool of self growth and self realization for the transformation of consciousness globally. The Seeds are a powerful catalyst of change, both for the individual and for the world. The Seeds have been given as a course that can lead you towards enlightenment. Each Seed contains within it a powerful packet of energy and information that is linked to the next Seed, thereby creating an ongoing and exciting discovery of the process of self realization.

By using each Seed for a week, you will be able to familiarize yourself with the depth of meaning and understanding that lies within that particular Seed. The Seeds can be used both within meditation as a mantra to focus and contemplate upon and also as a powerful thought form to be used throughout your day whilst in the midst of activity. With each new Seed take a few quiet moments to introduce it into your conscious and subconscious mind. Then throughout the week try to spend at least a few quiet moments every day working with that particular Seed and notice any thoughts, feelings, or memories that it evokes. Regular repetition and reminders throughout the day of which Seed you are working on will help it to penetrate deeper into the different layers of your mind.

As many people plant the Seeds in their consciousness, together they will create a powerful energy field, which extends from inside out. Gradually this energy field of love, compassion, and wisdom will begin to disintegrate the outer chaos, which we may currently perceive. In this way, change can be created through focused and directed attention. When many people put their attention regularly on the transformation of consciousness, extraordinary occurrences can take place. Using the Seeds of Transformation in this simple way enables us to not only uplift and transform our own lives, but also to assist in a global transformation through the elevation of consciousness that can move us in the direction of unity consciousness.

The Seeds are a gift from the Gods, appreciate them and nurture them well and share them with all those with whom you come into contact, and the rewards will be outstanding.

Maggie Erotokritou, Nicosia, Cyprus, January 2007

SEED I
HARMONY

———

HARMONY is the basic balancing principle that underlies everything. Where there is HARMONY, there is also a good energy flow. With HARMONY everything falls into place at the right time.

As you work with HARMONY, you begin to discern the difference between HARMONIOUS vibrations, which are beneficial and increase positive communication, and disharmonious vibrations, which are detrimental and create resistance or diminish your energy levels. Even the most subtle inharmonious vibrations can be destructive and prevent the manifestation of what you desire. You have to become increasingly more watchful that you give out only HARMONIOUS vibrations so as not to create any discord in your life. What you give out is what you will receive back.

Notice the different qualities between the HARMONIOUS softness of responding and the harshness of reaction. When you respond, you say yes to the universe and go with the flow instead of against it, like the tide that effortlessly comes in and out. In this way, you dispel harsh frequencies with HARMONIC vibrations. The process begins from within. You cannot be satisfied until all discord has been dispelled and you are able to continuously maintain an inner HARMONIOUS state.

Plant the thought of HARMONY in your consciousness and visualize the colour green in your heart chakra. Allow thoughts or pictures to come and go but don't get attached to them. Keep coming back to the thought of HARMONY. What does it mean to you and how do you see the manifestation of HARMONY within the world? How can being more HARMONIOUS change your life?

Think about HARMONY both in and out of meditation; keep it as an important focus in your mind throughout the week; make notes on your insights and at the end of the week reflect on what you have written and how important remaining HARMONIOUS is for you.

Reflections on
HARMONY
———

By working with HARMONY, you begin to create a more HARMONIOUS auric field and when this becomes strong enough, then no discordant energies can penetrate. HARMONY is respectful of others, it responds, allows, embraces, and transforms; it does not engage in discord in any form. HARMONY puts you in touch with yourself; it brings you closer to who you really are.

As the ripples of HARMONY spread out, they have a soothing, calming effect that unwinds tension and helps you to release. The green colour of HARMONY is gentle and nurturing, it soothes the nerves, calms ruffled feathers, and softens rough edges.

Where there is true HARMONY, there is no place for stress or strain. HARMONY is one of the first essential steps in any healing programme. By focusing on HARMONY, it brings to the surface whatever needs to be seen. The more you work with HARMONY, the more apparent it becomes how much disharmony and discord there is in the world. It is through becoming more HARMONIOUS within yourself that you can begin to create a more HARMONIC environment around you and return to a more HARMONIOUS way of living.

SEEDS *of* TRANSFORMATION

SEED 2
PEACE

———

As you remember the Seed harmony, and the harmonious state it brings, sit quietly and connect to the second Seed, PEACE. At this point don't think about what PEACE means, just try to get a sense or a feeling of PEACE within you. Move deeper within yourself to experience this. Don't let any sounds around you distract you from your inner PEACE. At the same time, visualize the palest sky blue all around you and feel this blue penetrating into every cell of your body. Allow yourself to become PEACE, to merge totally with it, to be PEACE.

Whenever you find your mind wandering, just think again upon the word PEACE. Let it be your mantra. Try to maintain the feeling of PEACE throughout your day and to become aware whenever you have been drawn away from it and try to regain that feeling of PEACE.

Keep thinking about PEACE throughout the day and for the following days to come; you will learn a lot about yourself during this process. Then think about the importance of inner PEACE and what it means to you and how it affects your outer environment and the collective thoughts on the planet.

Think about inner PEACE and outer PEACE and how they are one and the same.

Reflections on
PEACE

———

We live in a world where there is so much turmoil, but by working with PEACE, both in an inner and outer way, we can bring about change. Just like a pebble that is thrown into a pond and the ripples expand outwards from it, so are the effects of PEACE when it is planted in your consciousness. Creating PEACE in the world begins with creating PEACE within yourself. Then a hundredth monkey effect can be created, as PEACE spreads from person to person and gradually transforms the whole world.

Don't allow outer circumstances to disturb your inner PEACE. Don't get pulled into other people's chaos or dramas; maintain your inner PEACE wherever you go. PEACE is a starting point for something new. PEACE softens and breaks down resistances and opens the way to new possibilities. Become a PEACE maker and help transform the world.

SEED 3
STILLNESS

As you continue to hold harmony and peace in your consciousness, you create a more harmonious energy field. Then feelings of irritation and distress gradually begin to calm down and dissolve and you start to feel more relaxed even in the face of adversity and during periods of intense work. Learning to maintain this feeling of well-being is imperative to your health and for any level of healing that may be needed.

As you move deeper within yourself and begin to experience more calmness and get used to settling down into a more meditative state, you will discover a state of STILLNESS that is not disturbed by outer activity. At first you may have fleeting glimpses and only momentary experiences of STILLNESS, but as you persevere, it begins to infiltrate and pervade every area of your life.

STILLNESS can be breathtaking, for it contains everything within it, both that which is known and as yet unknown. As you bring more STILLNESS into your life, you also gain the ability to see in a new way, for it is in the moments of STILLNESS that so much is revealed.

Allow yourself to move deeper so you can quieten down and remain in STILLNESS. You don't have to do anything, just to be with the STILLNESS, to let it immerse, surround, and fill you up.

In the midst of action and before every meeting or event, remember to take a few moments of STILLNESS. Pause throughout the day to regain and maintain your equilibrium. Always come back to STILLNESS.

Reflections on
STILLNESS

STILLNESS refreshes us; it is like a good night's sleep. Become a silent observer, holding STILLNESS even in the midst of a storm, not allowing outer disturbances to affect your inner state of STILLNESS. It takes practice but as you will discover the benefits are enormous.

When you practise STILLNESS, you realize how powerful it is. In STILLNESS, you come to a place where you can attain the right frequency that brings you into a closer alignment both with yourself and everything around you.

Through STILLNESS, you can discover a depth that you can never forget because it opens you to new horizons; the remembrance of which is always there, gently reminding you somewhere in the background. STILLNESS empowers you to see more clearly what is needed. In STILLNESS you discover there is no need to rush or strain, everything has its natural unfoldment.

STILLNESS shows us the expansive energy of silence that is within us and offers to put us in touch with a healing power that is far more powerful than you can even begin to imagine. STILLNESS is there, waiting to be found.

SEEDS *of* TRANSFORMATION

BEING

———

As the blending of harmony, peace, and stillness occurs, you can sense the beginning of an inner transformation taking place. You can feel yourself gently moving into a new state of BEING that brings with it a freedom that is as yet unknown. This brings you a new understanding of where you have been and where you are going but at the same time invites you to remain resting in the dynamic presence of the moment. Discord of any kind has no place in BEING.

BEING allows, BEING welcomes, BEING is. From BEING emerges the wisdom of the ages and the power of the gods. BEING moves us closer to our essence, to our true self in its infinite wisdom and potential as the veils of misconception are removed. Move into BEING and rest there quietly, allowing the discovery of who you really are.

From BEING, you can review your life, see what you have created and what you want to create or gain insights into how you might now do things differently. The outer is a reflection of the inner. As you make changes on the inner levels, a new reality will be reflected in the outer.

[1 8]

Reflections on
BEING

In BEING, you discover what needs attention; you watch the movement, the fluctuations, and the ups and downs of life. You observe the tenderness and the cruelty, the joy and the pain, the exhilaration and the disappointment. Gradually you learn how to distinguish and remain unaffected by the outer processes, not untouched but unscathed.

From BEING all is revealed. Through observing the process of birth, death, and rebirth, you come to understand how the outer form may change; yet your innermost core, your essence, remains the same. In BEING you also discover the need for purification and release, the letting go of anything that interferes with your connection to your true essence. BEING shows what has clouded your vision or restricted the full expression of who you truly are. BEING opens the way and leads you to freedom and connectedness.

SEED 5

RELEASE

———

From a centred state of being, immersed in stillness, you start to gain a new perspective on life. You see what no longer serves you, what binds and holds you back, and you become aware of what you need to RELEASE. You recognize discord as it occurs and can now choose to step back and detach from it, affirming that negativity, discord, and conflict no longer have any place in your life.

All the emotional baggage from the past needs to be cut free and RELEASED. It weighs too much; it takes your energy, drags you down, and prevents you from moving forward. RELEASE helps you cut the cords from the past so you are able to move on. RELEASE clears the way and opens the door for something new to come in. As you peel away and RELEASE the layers of guilt, resentment, and fear, a new clarity emerges.

From an empowered state within, command the RELEASE of what you need to let go of. A clear space is desired now that has no place for lingering, haunting memories from the past. It is time to free yourself through RELEASE so that your true self, which is without limitations, can emerge.

Hold the thought of RELEASE in your consciousness and remember it throughout the day as things occur. Don't hold onto anything, and don't let things build up, for it is the accumulation of things that creates deeper problems. The more you stay centred in clear space, in being, the more you will understand the necessity of RELEASE.

Reflections on
RELEASE

—

RELEASE is an ongoing process; you cannot RELEASE everything in one go, but you can gradually peel back the layers one by one, letting go of anything that no longer serves your present state of being. The more you work with RELEASE, the more you realize how much you have been holding in your body and what the effects of that are upon your mind, emotional state, energy levels, and the consequences they have had upon your life. RELEASE needs a lot of attention until you feel clear enough.

Throughout the day, become more attentive and watchful; if old resentments emerge again or negative thoughts come up, RELEASE them, do not give them energy. You may discover layers and layers of judgements, rigid structures, old patterns, and conditioning that have accumulated over the years: all of these need to be RELEASED. See them as sticky matter, which has got stuck in your auric field or in your body and as you RELEASE these old patterns, you will feel so much lighter. Then with practice you will be able to quickly let go and to easily repel any negative or derogatory thought forms that don't serve your highest level of evolvement. Peel them off, day by day, like dried up old scabs that need to be removed. As you RELEASE these old thought forms that no longer serve you, see them being transformed into light particles by the rays of the sun.

The more you work with RELEASE, the more you realize just how much you have been holding. RELEASE is a very powerful cleansing process and is an essential part of your journey of self development.

SEED 6
VISION

——

When you begin the process of clearing your internal space, you start to get a sense of something new. You feel hope, and the feeling of trust develops as you start to see glimmers of light at the end of the tunnel. Release moves you through the fog of deception into the realms of light. You realize you have a choice and you can choose to discard that which no longer serves you in order to make space for something better to come in. This is an important step in your transformational process and assists you in gaining a new perspective.

VISION asks you to see in a new way, from a clearer space, and to disregard that which you thought you knew. VISION asks you to stay open. VISION offers you a more refined perception; it is a gift from the divine. Through VISION, you start to break through. VISION is the first step of seeing on the road to enlightenment. As you start to see differently, you gain clarity and understanding about many things and this propels you forward in a more focused and determined way. VISION helps you to see more clearly what needs to be done.

In meditation, whilst focusing your awareness on the area of the third eye, the centre of the frontal part of the brain, plant the Seed of VISION and allow whatever needs to come forward to be seen. Keep your attention focused on this area.

Throughout the week, both in and out of meditation, hold your focus on VISION and allow a whole new perspective for your life to emerge.

Reflections on
VISION

———

As you focus on VISION, many things start popping into your mind and new ideas start formulating. Now that you know the value of not suppressing or holding onto anything from the past, VISION will present that which still needs to be seen. You will experience an inner shift, which assists your new way of seeing and then you will find yourself looking at everything in a new way.

VISION and release work go hand in hand. VISION asks you to see, whereas release asks you to let go of what you have seen in the past. VISION shows you how to look deeper and teaches you how to develop your skills of seeing. VISION then refines everything you see by further expanding your perception.

VISION urges you to create a better quality of life and shows you step by step how to do this. VISION moves you in the direction of truth and fulfilment and shows you what is possible. VISION also shows you where you have held yourself back and where your fears and insecurities lie. VISION leads you through the mist as the clouds begin to drift apart.

Recognize where your VISION has been clouded and where you were previously unable to see, as if walking in the dark; but now the way is opening and you can see the light. VISION develops the ability to see clearly, without bias and without judgement. From being, VISION gives you an entirely new perspective and then understanding dawns.

SEED 7

UNDERSTANDING

Out of vision emerges UNDERSTANDING, and glimmers of the truth begin to filter through. What you have always known but maybe not recognized becomes more visible. You are able to see what was always there and how things really are, rather than your previous limited interpretation of how you thought things were. Vision parts the veils so that truth can step forward. Vision gives you new insights and new ways of looking at things that help you to improve your UNDERSTANDING.

In UNDERSTANDING, you begin to experience the "aha syndrome" and the feelings of *déjà vu*. "Aha" is a response that means you recognize something, you finally get it, you UNDERSTAND. Then you wonder what has taken you so long, why you floundered around and lacked UNDERSTANDING. As your vision gives you more clarity, UNDERSTANDING comes easily.

UNDERSTANDING sets you free because when you UNDERSTAND, you are no longer locked into the past; you have released it, gained vision, and can move forward and make better choices that enhance your life.

Reflections on
UNDERSTANDING
———

There are many levels of UNDERSTANDING. Through UNDER-STANDING, you gain recognition of what has been, and how and why things have evolved in the way they have and what you can now do differently.

You recognize how you have created your present reality, and if there is still confusion, you are urged to look deeper to find your answers. UNDERSTANDING shows you how the culmination of certain events and experiences brought you to this point in time. If you wish to move in a new direction or make changes, then you have to look at how you can actively make certain preparations in order to change course.

Sometimes it only requires a simple shift of one degree to start moving in a new direction, whereas on the other hand, sometimes a major shift or life change is actually required. This is for you to UNDERSTAND according to your present life circumstances and level of consciousness, and for the attainment of your goals and desires. Some things may take longer to UNDERSTAND but everything comes at the right time.

SEED 8
REVIEW

———

There will be times during the course when it is good to take a break, to pause and reflect on the work that has been done and the Seeds that have been planted so far.

The eighth Seed, REVIEW gives you the time to do this, to spend a whole week REVIEWING what has been learnt so far. It is important not to skip over this REVIEW, but to see it as an opportunity to reflect and ponder on your experiences of the Seeds so far.

The REVIEW also gives you time to integrate the learning acquired over the last few weeks and to become aware of the delicate thread that links the Seeds together.

REFLECTIONS

Take one day of the week to review each of the following Seeds.

Day 1
HARMONY: this is the Seed that was planted in your heart. Experience again the waves of HARMONIOUS green energy.

Day 2
PEACE: feel pale blue energy surrounding you and permeating every cell of your body. Think about inner and outer PEACE.

Day 3
STILLNESS: by combining harmony and peace move deeper into STILLNESS.

Day 4
BEING: move into the deepest level of your BEING to discover more about who you really are.

Day 5
RELEASE: discover what else you need to RELEASE.

Day 6
VISION: as the clouds part, VISION emerges.

Day 7
UNDERSTANDING: and then UNDERSTANDING becomes clearer. What else do you need to UNDERSTAND?

Which Seed needs the most attention or nurturing? Keep it in mind as you work with the next cycle of transformation.

SEED 9
DEPTH

———

As you reviewed the previous Seeds that you have already worked with, you may have discovered that your experiences went deeper than the first time you encountered each Seed. You probably also realized that there is still the need to go even DEEPER.

In planting the Seed DEPTH, there is a remembering, a rekindling of what we already know but may have forgotten. In reviewing past situations or with every new situation that presents itself, you are asked to move DEEPER, to explore and acquire a DEPTH that you may never have reached before.

With DEPTH, you will be able to discern what has real meaning and value for you and what does not. This will help you see through the superficial guises that try to draw your attention and energy. Through DEPTH, you can embrace what is real and draw to you that which will really fulfil you. This will encourage you to let go of what no longer serves you and to focus on realizing your highest potential. Through DEPTH, you can attain the DEEPEST and the highest.

DEPTH asks you to look DEEPER at everything in your life in order to ascertain what is of value and what is not. DEPTH brings you closer to the truth and helps you find what you are looking for. DEPTH asks you to look again and to keep looking, DEEPER and DEEPER, until you find the answers you are searching for.

Reflections on
DEPTH
———

DEPTH takes you to a new level. It helps you move beyond what had previously seemed impassable. DEPTH helps you gain a new perspective and opens you to a more expansive way of seeing. DEPTH shows you there is always more to learn. DEPTH and understanding go hand in hand, they embrace each other. You go a little DEEPER and you understand even more. The spiral of revelation is ongoing.

DEPTH teaches you to be more open and to put aside your fixed ideas and beliefs, and to be aware of something more. DEPTH takes you into the source of your being, where everything waits patiently to be revealed.

SEED 10

REFINEMENT

The Seed REFINEMENT refers to the subtle awareness of one's self and one's life and the manner in which you conduct your life. REFINEMENT lifts your awareness to another level, which creates a shift in frequency. Your current frequency is determined by the vibrations you give out. Now you are being asked to REFINE those vibrations and to bring them into alignment with a much higher frequency to create a quantum shift in your life.

REFINEMENT brings an awareness of the quality of life you desire and how your present vibrational level may not yet match with that which you wish to attain. Attention needs to be given to what you give out, for like attracts like. There may still be a need to soothe rough edges or to dissolve harshness or ease tautness so you can move into a state of effortless being. REFINEMENT may require releasing tension, frustration, or anger, which still hover in the bodymind consciousness, so that these feelings can be replaced by more harmonious and peaceful vibrations.

There needs to be more REFINEMENT in all of your expressions, from the subtle to the mundane, in both the spiritual and physical realms. REFINEMENT indicates to you what changes need to be made, subtle or otherwise, in order to keep improving yourself. REFINEMENT encourages you to take note of the details, for sometimes it is the REFINEMENT of the smallest details that can make the difference in whether something is successful or not. REFINEMENT is a quality that allows a new kind of perception and experience that adds depth, value, and meaning to your life.

Reflections on
REFINEMENT

REFINEMENT occurs on many levels and it is an ongoing process. Sometimes even a tiny shift can make all the difference. REFINEMENT is also part of the process of rebalancing and realigning, which brings you back to your natural state of being, who you truly are and who you can become. Through REFINEMENT, you begin to get a sense of the God presence within you and how you can come even closer to the sacred state of oneness, which is omnipresent and omnipotent.

REFINEMENT is subtle and requires the full functioning of the senses. REFINEMENT is a fine tuning tool that sharpens your observation skills and awareness. Through REFINEMENT you recognize how much work there is still to be done and that this can be accomplished with joy instead of judgement. REFINEMENT asks you to go deeper rather than just skimming over the surface.

REFINEMENT invites you to enjoy a higher quality of life, one that is truly fulfilling, through living your truth from the highest level of integrity.

SEED 11
REFINED SIGHT

As you start to explore refinement, you are also asked to work with refining the senses. The first sense to work with is REFINED SIGHT.

As your SIGHT REFINES you start to look at everything differently, you realize that nothing is as you thought it was before. Not only do you now see deeper and clearer, but you also realize that there are many ways to see things, according to where you are seeing from and whether it is from a balanced and harmonious state.

As the veils part, the truth becomes more obvious. REFINED SIGHT moves you through the illusions into the light. You are able to look beyond the obvious to the profound and you do not allow the superficial to influence you because you see through it. You live more from being and therefore can understand and express what is there in the moment. Being fully in the present enables you to create a better future; one that you may not have previously envisioned.

With REFINED SIGHT nothing will ever be the same, for it is continuously REFINING. You will see with new eyes, and both your inner and outer vision will be so changed. Look for the beauty and the joy that is all around you: it is there, just waiting to be found.

REFINED SIGHT enables you to see with the innocence of a child, without prejudice or judgement; then the impossible becomes possible and the self-constructed boundaries and limitations fall away.

Reflections on
REFINED SIGHT

With each day that passes, there is yet another opportunity to REFINE your SIGHT, to look again and to see what you could not see before. There is always a new perspective to be gained or a new way to look at things. REFINED SIGHT gives you the opportunity to experiment with different tinted lenses.

Who you were yesterday is not who you are today and tomorrow you will change yet again. REFINED SIGHT shows you how everything is constantly shifting and changing, and how there is always so much more to be seen as you discover how to look deeper and move beyond past conditioning.

REFINED SIGHT gives you the chance to look at everyone as if it is the first time you are meeting, from a clear space, without prejudice or judgements. REFINED SIGHT invites you to create new relationships and to interact in a different way.

REFINED SIGHT helps you redefine how you live your life and accordingly gives you insights into what is really important and meaningful. REFINED SIGHT shows you how to enjoy the beauty of life by opening to what stands before you.

SEED 12
REFINED HEARING

REFINED HEARING asks you to listen in a different way and to be more attentive to the other person whilst listening. This requires being genuinely interested rather than being wrapped up in yourself and your present needs. The ego wants all the attention, it doesn't want to listen. How often do you switch off and not want to HEAR? When you do that, it disconnects the communication and the other person feels unheard.

At the same time REFINED HEARING asks you to listen carefully to your internal dialogue and the messages you receive. If you do not listen properly, you cannot act on the internal guidance that you are given.

REFINED HEARING allows you to HEAR beyond the words, even to what is not being said or to the authenticity of what is being said. REFINED HEARING also allows you to distinguish when a person is speaking from their ego, their mind, or their heart and soul.

As you move into the silence and into the stillness, you realize that silence is not quiet. For there in the depths of your being, through REFINED HEARING you can HEAR the universal hum, the sound of the cosmic OM, which is so beautiful it takes your breath away.

In the depths of silence, using REFINED HEARING, everything can be HEARD.

Reflections on
REFINED HEARING

REFINED HEARING gives you the opportunity to listen in a deeper way. As you pay more attention, you notice that you are becoming aware of things you had not been aware of before. REFINED HEARING is like being finely tuned, the tone is different and you realize you can tune into different channels, and your scope is wider.

REFINED HEARING helps to create an even balance between speaking and listening. You realize the value of listening more carefully. REFINED HEARING allows you to get to know others better. You can go beyond the words and just from the tone of someone's voice you can come to know many things about them. So much that is not actually said can be understood from the tone of someone's voice. There could be a slight edge or sharpness, anger, abruptness, or expressions of kindness or love.

REFINED HEARING is profoundly useful in any exchange. The underlying messages become clearer when you pay attention and really listen. Make a point to be still, to move into being and to listen with every cell of your body. You will be surprised at how much more you HEAR.

Listen to the sounds around you, to the sounds of nature, the birds greeting you in the morning, the whisper of the wind as it blows through the trees. Listen to the plants, the rocks, and the earth; each has a story to tell.

Listen to the sounds of your own body, your breathing, your heart beating, the blood flowing through your veins, the different sounds that each organ makes. REFINED HEARING enables you to know yourself deeply, and enables you to HEAR the sound of creation, the I AM and the all that is.

SEED 13
REFINED TOUCH

REFINED TOUCH is very subtle; it requires presence, gentleness, and tenderness. It is nourishing and supportive; it is sensual and sensitive. Everyone needs to TOUCH and be TOUCHED yet we live in a time when TOUCH is so easily misunderstood and this often makes us afraid to TOUCH.

REFINED TOUCH soothes the pain of the heart; it speaks of caring and love, yet it can be both personal and impersonal. REFINED TOUCH gives us a sense of what is; it sends messages to the brain, which have a deep healing effect. REFINED TOUCH requires a deep level of sensitivity and being in tune with where the other person is so you know whether it is safe to TOUCH or not. Whether TOUCHING a person, an object, a plant, or an animal, there is a connection, and a communication that does not necessarily need words because REFINED TOUCH speaks for itself.

Through REFINED TOUCH energy exchanges occur, and shifts take place within the body, which help bring the bodymind back to balance. REFINED TOUCH can take you back to childhood, back to a time when you felt safe and secure. Through REFINED TOUCH there is a giving and a receiving, a sharing and an exchange. REFINED TOUCH creates a deep interaction that brings about change.

Reflections on
REFINED TOUCH

As you go deeper, you see how important REFINED TOUCH is as a means of communication. REFINED TOUCH can express friendship and caring or be an indication of support. REFINED TOUCH can also put you in TOUCH with the soul of a person because through TOUCH you can get glimpses of what lies hidden beneath the surface. REFINED TOUCH can release that which is locked inside. A handshake, a gentle tap on the shoulder, a pat on the back, a hug, a warm caress; all can offer the much needed contact or the opportunity for release and healing.

The more you become aware of your own feelings around REFINED TOUCH, the more you will understand the needs of others as well. The body speaks, it wants to be heard, and REFINED TOUCH gives the body a way to respond. In any treatment you go for, massage, healing, BodyTalk, or other TOUCH oriented therapeutic modalities, be aware of the TOUCH and vibrations of the person who is working on you; if it doesn't feel good, either choose to stop the treatment or don't go again. Be selective about who you allow to work on you.

Your body knows and will respond to that which is loving and caring and to the higher vibrations, which can be transmitted through REFINED TOUCH. Always trust your intuition; you know best what is good for you.

SEED 14
REFINED SMELL

———

There is an important connection between REFINED SMELL and memory. REFINED SMELL can trigger memories of people and places. REFINED SMELL can take you back to childhood, and even further back to the remembrance of your mother's milk and the connection to being deeply nourished. The more REFINED the sense of SMELL, the deeper the memories you can access.

REFINED SMELL will naturally make you more aware of which SMELLS are pleasing to you or which are unpleasant and those which you find less desirable. You will notice some SMELLS bring back pleasant memories, whereas others remind you of unpleasant experiences.

REFINED SMELL can trigger the SMELL of things you enjoy or love, home baked bread and biscuits, freshly picked fruits, your favourite foods, the SMELL of the earth after it rains, freshly cut grass, and the salty SMELL of the sea, all of which connect you to certain places, times in your life, and people that you associate with those times. REFINED SMELL can trigger many visual experiences too.

REFINED SMELL makes you aware that different SMELLS evoke different moods, for example, essential oils and incense can influence both your emotions and hormones and some may be pleasing, whereas others may repel. Essential oils can be spicy and invigorating, sensual or relaxing, or they may calm or energize. REFINED SMELL makes you more aware of the perfumes, creams, and oils you use on your body and whether they nourish and make you feel good.

REFINED SMELL asks you to pay attention to your own SMELL and this will let you know if you are toxic or unbalanced. REFINED SMELL draws your attention to the SMELLS around you, including in your home and workspace and to become aware of how these might affect or influence you.

Through REFINED SMELL you become aware of why you are more attracted to some people rather than others. Everyone has their own unique SMELL; it is said that you are actually attracted to someone because of their particular SMELL, their sensual/sexual aroma, and not their visual appearance as you might think. REFINED SMELL makes you aware of the body chemistry between people and whether this attracts or repels.

Reflections on
REFINED SMELL

The olfactory system, which senses and processes SMELLS, is one of the vital parts of the brain. Animals have a much stronger sense of SMELL than humans; it is their primary mode of communication. They SMELL when danger is near. With REFINED SMELL you can also develop this sense so that it tells you when something is not right or danger is imminent, which enables you to avoid it or to be more prepared.

REFINED SMELL can also give you the sense of whether to trust someone or not. Your sense of SMELL can recognize when someone is lying or trying to do something dishonest. It is their bodily SMELL that tells you; people get nervous when doing something that is not right and this produces certain hormones. If your sense of SMELL is REFINED enough, you can pick it up.

The sense of SMELL affects your thoughts, emotions, and behaviour; it can evoke many images and sensations, so make sure to have the right kind of beneficial SMELLS around you, both in your home and workspace. Also be aware of which products that you choose to use on your body: the senses desire to be pleased in the right way.

If the nasal passages are blocked, this can affect the neurological connections in the brain. Many people have a poor sense of SMELL due to smoking or taking other substances that dull the senses. Yogic pranayama breathing techniques are powerful ways to stimulate the brain and help clear the nasal passages; this can improve and REFINE your sense of SMELL.

SEED 15
REFINED TASTE

———

As soon as you think of TASTE, the first thing that comes to mind is food. Foods that you like to eat and bring pleasure to the palate and also foods that you dislike. TASTE also evokes memories including childhood memories that are connected to food, and associations with mealtimes and whether these experiences were pleasant or unpleasant, relaxed or tense.

The whole process of food and eating is a highly emotional subject, and people get very attached to their food patterns. We see the difficulties people have when they try to diet or to give up certain foods and how much resistance comes up. People may feel emotionally deprived or depressed because they have associated pleasure or emotional nourishment with particular foods, regardless of whether that food is actually nourishing for them or not. It is the association with a particular food or eating in general that needs to be addressed in order to break the pattern of attachment. The sense of TASTE remembers the temporary pleasure, and in this way addictions are created, especially when you are feeling emotionally low or stressed.

REFINED TASTE shows you that food and the process of eating is not just about what satisfies you emotionally, but that food should be seen as substances that nourish, revitalize, and nurture your body and therefore increases your whole feeling of well-being. REFINED TASTE will make you more aware when your emotional needs are overriding the real needs of your body.

REFINED TASTE draws you towards that which is *sattvic*. *Sattvic* is a Sanskrit word meaning pure, refined, and wholesome. *Sattvic* foods create balance and healing. When your TASTE becomes more REFINED, your taste buds will become more REFINED too and this will diminish any cravings for unhealthy foods and substances.

Reflections on
REFINED TASTE

REFINED TASTE ensures that you attract that which is enriching and nourishing into your life. With REFINED TASTE you desire only that which is for your highest good, including the foods you eat and any substances that you take into your body.

What you desire and what TASTES good to you reflects where you are in your life and this can evolve and change with time as your needs and desires change, and as your TASTE becomes more REFINED. Add new flavours to your life and notice how your TASTE of life begins to change and don't be afraid to experiment.

REFINED TASTE helps you become aware of the subtler aspects of life. The most REFINED TASTE that you can be aware of is the TASTE of life. Sweetness brings joy, whereas sourness brings unhappiness, and resentment and bitterness lead to disappointment and depression. Choose sweetness and savour the good things in life.

SEED 16
REFINED INTUITION

REFINED INTUITION is also known as the sixth sense, and its development depends upon the refinement of the other senses. REFINED INTUITION combines the clarity of refined sight, the aptitude to listen deeply through refined hearing, the ability to get a feel for things through refined touch, and to sense what is going on through refined smell and refined taste. The more the five senses are developed, the sharper your REFINED INTUITION will become.

REFINED INTUITION also relies on the ability to process and assimilate the information that is being received. The mind needs to be open to receive new ideas and concepts, otherwise it will reject the information that is given if it is beyond the conscious knowing and awareness of the receiver. This is why people often receive glimpses and insights, but they may dismiss them or not act upon them because they do not trust or understand what they are receiving.

REFINED INTUITION needs the refinement of both the left and right sides of the brain. REFINED INTUITION is not just a right brained phenomenon as some people may think. It involves the balanced interaction of the left and right sides of the brain. Knowledge, information, and structure need to be combined with deep right brained processing in order for assimilation and creative expression to take place. REFINED INTUITION can take you into the higher realms so you can access the required information and process it in the right way.

Reflections on
REFINED INTUITION

The more you are able to remain in stillness and in being, even in the midst of activity, the easier you will be able to access your REFINED INTUITION at any time. This is described as being in the zone. The zone is an area beyond space and time from where you can connect to the higher dimensions, and gain access to information previously unknown and beyond your present awareness.

With practice and attention, your skills of REFINING your INTUITION will improve and you will be able to access the information you require easily. Through learning to pay attention and listen with the whole of your being, this will bring you into a closer communion with life.

REFINED INTUITION will open you to new possibilities as you realize that nothing is by chance and that everything is divinely orchestrated according to your ability to know, perceive, and understand and your willingness to act spontaneously upon the information you are given. REFINED INTUITION will direct you to be in the right place at the right time and to recognize that other elements are also at work bringing you the necessary assistance that is needed. REFINED INTUITION can greatly enhance your work, no matter what your field of interest may be.

REFINED INTUITION teaches you to be patient and to wait until the time is right, and that there is a right time for everything. REFINED INTUITION reminds you to stay in the present moment, to grasp the power of the now, to be with what is, as you watch the unfoldment of what is becoming and what can be.

Allow REFINED INTUITION to guide you in everything you do.

SEED 17
PAUSE

Take time to pause and reflect on the recent Seeds that you have been working with and to see the thread that connects them.

Which Seeds still need more attention?

SEED 9 – DEPTH

SEED 10 – REFINEMENT

SEED 11 – REFINED SIGHT

SEED 12 – REFINED HEARING

SEED 13 – REFINED TOUCH

SEED 14 – REFINED SMELL

SEED 15 – REFINED TASTE

SEED 16 – REFINED INTUITION

REFLECTIONS

As I become more aware, I REFINE all my senses.

I have REFINED SIGHT. I SEE more clearly.

I have REFINED HEARING. I HEAR more acutely.

I have REFINED TOUCH. I can sense through TOUCH.

I have REFINED SMELL. I know which SMELLS are nourishing
for me.

I have REFINED TASTE. I am attracted to *sattvic* TASTES.

I have REFINED INTUITION. I am guided by my
REFINED INTUITION.

SEED 18
VIBRATION

Everything has a VIBRATION and VIBRATES on some level. There are different qualities of VIBRATION, some are high and some are low. Higher VIBRATIONS nourish and support, whereas lower VIBRATIONS drain and tire. Through the development of refined intuition, you will become more aware of the VIBRATIONS that you give out, as well as the VIBRATIONS around you, and those that you attract and receive.

Being able to discern the different quality of VIBRATION is essential for your well-being and protection. This will also increase your awareness of what resonates with you and what doesn't. People VIBRATE on different levels, so choose carefully who you spend your time with and notice afterwards whether you feel uplifted or if your energy feels low or depleted because some people can drain your energy. You will also notice how different places have different VIBRATIONS and the effects that they have upon you. It is not by chance that most sensitive people are drawn to nature, to places in the wilderness, or to certain sacred places where the energy is higher. Higher VIBRATIONS replenish and purify and lift you up.

The VIBRATIONS that you surround yourself with and what you draw to you are in direct accordance and alignment with the VIBRATIONS that you give out. If you are having difficulty in manifesting the life you wish to create and you feel you deserve a better quality of life, then be consciously aware of the quality of VIBRATION you give out, for life is a mirror and like attracts like. What you sow, you reap.

The more aware you are of your own VIBRATION and what you are giving out, the easier it will be to make the necessary changes in your life to create the circumstances that you desire. Every VIBRATION has a boomerang effect. If you send out VIBRATIONS such as anger, resentment, or discontent, it will be reflected back to you, whereas if you send out VIBRATIONS of love and appreciation with the spirit of joy and goodwill, then this is what you will receive back.

You are the creator of your reality and your VIBRATIONS create the energy patterns for whatever you wish to attract.

Reflections on
VIBRATION

VIBRATIONS are like ripples in the pond, they begin from a central point within you and their effects radiate out and are felt by those who are within close proximity to you and within your circle of influence and even further afield. You are always working within the parameters of cause and effect. If you don't like the outcome of something and the overall effect, then look deeper within yourself to see what the cause of the discomfort or disturbance really might be and where it comes from.

The higher the level of evolvement and the higher the VIBRATION you give out, then the quicker the corresponding response occurs. Remember the boomerang effect and make sure you send out only that which you would wish to receive. If there are still blocked emotions or old patterns from the past that are keeping you stuck, you may need to go back and work again with the Seed release so you can clear those emotions and set yourself free and lift your VIBRATION to a higher level.

Be conscious of the VIBRATION that you hold most of the time and the quality of your thoughts throughout the day. Is your VIBRATION peaceful, harmonious, and joyful, or is it a lower VIBRATION that interferes and disturbs your energy level and prevents you from moving forward?

Your VIBRATION is your personal signature; it represents who you are. Is this in alignment with who you know yourself to be in the depths of your inner being? Your VIBRATION is the expression of your present consciousness, so you need to be acutely aware of what you are holding in your consciousness.

SEED 19

CONTEMPLATION

———

The Seed of CONTEMPLATION encompasses so many of the previous states. In order to move into a state of CONTEMPLATION, harmony, inner peace, stillness, and an understanding of being are required. CONTEMPLATION is a state wherein you quietly and peacefully reflect upon something. This could be a subject, which you wish to gain a deeper understanding about or to gain a new perspective; or it could be something new, which as yet you have limited knowledge about but would like to explore deeper.

CONTEMPLATION allows you to access that which is beyond the conscious mind. You take the facts, the insights and use your refined intuition to explore further. CONTEMPLATION opens you to a wider perspective of what is possible and opens the way to a clarity that you may not have previously considered possible. CONTEMPLATION takes you into the realms of the unlimited and the miraculous, where you can expand and enhance your whole vision of life. CONTEMPLATION gives you access to the potential that exists but is still in an unmanifest form.

In CONTEMPLATION you may wish to ponder upon the bigger picture of life and what your true life's purpose is and whether you are living it. This helps you to open to your full potential and to become more conscious of your direction rather than just floating through life. CONTEMPLATION can give you a sense of the greater whole and the important part you have to play within it.

You may CONTEMPLATE on anything that has importance to you and your life. Whatever you choose to CONTEMPLATE upon, you will discover that CONTEMPLATION is one of the most useful tools on your journey of discovery and awakening.

Reflections on
CONTEMPLATION

—

CONTEMPLATION is a way to come closer to yourself and to observe your life, as well as getting a sense of the greater whole. In CONTEMPLATION you take quiet time for yourself so that whatever is needed can surface from the unconscious. CONTEMPLATION also gives you access into the transpersonal realms.

CONTEMPLATION develops clarity and vision as it opens new doors that lead to a conscious awareness of the unfoldment of life, with all its gifts and treasures. CONTEMPLATION gives you the opportunity to see deeply, to move beyond the known, and to pierce through the veils of illusion.

CONTEMPLATION is action within stillness. CONTEMPLATION is active meditation, and it can help you see what is truly of value and importance in your life. The process of CONTEMPLATION is limitless; anything can be a subject for CONTEMPLATION.

With practice, life itself, and every glorious moment of life, can become an ongoing process of CONTEMPLATION.

SEED 20

FOCUS

Through contemplation, you realize the importance of FOCUS, of one pointed concentration. FOCUS brings the awareness of the need to harness the mind, to direct and train it. FOCUS is the process of unwavering concentration, of the ability to FOCUS on the task at hand, not allowing your mind to lose its concentration or sense of direction or to be distracted elsewhere.

FOCUS is a like a laser beam, it pierces through obstacles and limitations, and it helps you to stay with something even when the going seems hard. FOCUS pushes you through those difficult moments and draws your creativity to the surface; it helps you draw upon all the resources at hand.

FOCUS teaches you the art of mastery, that with consistent FOCUS, you can achieve anything you desire.

Reflections on
FOCUS

———

FOCUS opens the way; it parts the veils. FOCUS demands your full attention, whereas if you allow your mind to wander, the FOCUS is lost. FOCUS is a valuable process of mind training. FOCUS keeps your intent upon your priority; it reminds you of what is important in the moment. FOCUS prevents you from procrastinating; it helps you to get the job done.

FOCUS is like a guardian at the door, watching your mind, encouraging it to maintain its attention. FOCUS is a reminder that if you stay in line with what you are trying to achieve, you are bound to succeed. FOCUS will help you in every area of your life.

In meditation FOCUS takes you deeper; it pierces through to the truth, to that which lies beyond and it enables you to reach your ultimate goal.

SEED 21
INTENTION

The power behind focus is your INTENTION, knowing what you want, what you want to do, and what you are working towards. Then continuing to hold the INTENTION, even if the going gets hard or nothing seems to be happening yet.

INTENTION requires clarity; INTENTION and vagueness do not go together. If you don't hold a clear INTENTION in your mind, you won't know where to focus, whereas INTENTION will lead you directly towards your goal.

When your INTENTION is clear, your focus becomes stronger and you are able to create the reality that you desire. INTENTION leaves nothing to chance.

Reflections on
INTENTION

———

INTENTION implies that you have an idea or a plan, which you are ready to put into action. You may not know the exact details of this plan yet or how you are going to bring it into manifestation, but the clarity of INTENTION will draw to you the circumstances, people, and events that will help you achieve whatever you wish to do. The energy of INTENTION brings all the pieces of the jigsaw together.

Whatever you hold in your conscious mind is your INTENT. INTEND to be successful in what you are doing and you will be. INTENTION helps you to remain focused on the job at hand, so there can be no contradictions. If your mind is split between two or more options regarding one particular goal, then your INTENTION is not yet clear.

Lead an INTENTIONAL life by consciously creating your life, day by day, moment by moment. Be clear on where you want to go and you will surely arrive.

SEED 22

FLEXIBILITY

FLEXIBILTY teaches us to be on our toes all the time, to be alert and awake, for change is always in the air. Just when you think you know the way or you have the answers, the universe may deal you an unexpected hand. If you are FLEXIBILE enough, this will not throw you off course; you will take whatever appears in your stride and see it as yet another opportunity to strengthen your inner resolve and make any necessary adjustments that are required.

Anything can change at any time, life is so unpredictable, but FLEXIBILTY helps you to flow with life and move through the ups and downs with ease. If you are willing to be FLEXIBILE and to explore the different terrains, the known and the unknown, the high peaks and the valleys, you will travel an interesting and rewarding journey.

Just as you settle into your comfort zone, life may ask you to move on and explore something new. FLEXIBILTY will help you to make that move and show you the value of what is being presented. Those who are resistant to change struggle the most. They don't want to leave their comfort zone, but after a while that place may become stagnant and boring, a place which no longer supports your personal growth. Then you know it is time to move on.

A lack of FLEXIBILTY will keep you stuck in the same place, going round and round in circles and wondering why nothing new or exciting is happening in your life. On the other hand, FLEXIBILTY will always bring you something new.

Reflections on
FLEXIBILITY

FLEXIBILTY helps you stand strong in the face of adversity. With FLEXIBILTY, when the wind blows, you may bend but not break. With FLEXIBILTY you can remain well balanced and harmonious, and at the same time allow inner and outer changes to take place.

Focus and intention give you a sense of direction, they help you chart a course; but then FLEXIBILTY may require that you shift a few degrees or even make a complete turn when it is necessary. Sometimes we swim in unchartered waters and cannot yet see the horizon, but with focus, intention, and FLEXIBILTY you will reach your desired destination.

FLEXIBILTY asks you not to become set in your ways but to keep an open mind and to always stay alert for the unexpected. FLEXIBILTY also brings to you the most wonderful opportunities, things you could not begin to conceive.

FLEXIBILTY is the guiding force that pushes you through the difficult moments. FLEXIBILTY asks you to remain present and to be aware of both your inner state and present outer circumstances, remembering that you can always create and recreate in any given moment and that every day presents new opportunities, which will help you to achieve your desires.

SEED 23
PATIENCE

Again and again we are told that PATIENCE is a virtue, but it is one of the qualities that most of us find hard to consistently practise. We want things right now and in the way we want; but things come at the right time when they are meant to and often you just have to wait until things fall into place. The universe will not be hurried.

PATIENCE requires a peaceful state of being. PATIENCE asks you to be flexible. With PATIENCE all things are revealed, and sometimes when you have to wait, you discover that things are not the way you thought after all. PATIENCE helps you to gain clarity, for it is in the waiting that you start to see things you might not have otherwise recognized.

PATIENCE shows us the perfect synchronicity of life, that there is a right time for everything. The sun rises and sets when it is supposed to, the moon waxes and wanes at certain times of the month. Nature sleeps and awakens at the appropriate times. And so it is with everything in life. The universal forces are constantly at play; they wait for you to be ready and if you are not, they will wait PATIENTLY until you are. If there are lessons for you to learn first, then mountains will not move until those lessons have been learnt. You have to make friends with PATIENCE and allow life to unfold in its right time.

Reflections on
PATIENCE

There are times in our lives when there is intense activity, and at other times things are quieter and nothing much seems to be happening. This could be through the choices you have made or it could be because outer circumstances are not yet right for things to come together. PATIENCE helps you move through these times without your feathers getting ruffled. This does not mean you should be passive. You need to continue holding your intention and focus upon what you desire, knowing with certainty that things will unfold at the right moment and then they most certainly will.

PATIENCE is a teacher of many lessons that will test you again and again to see how alert and attentive you are. The tide may turn suddenly so you have to be ready and prepared, for you may be called to take action at any moment. When PATIENCE asks you to wait, you need to use your time wisely, seeing what else you can do in the meantime to prepare yourself and advance your evolvement. PATIENCE can be with you every step along the path if you invite it into your life. Nothing is by chance and nothing is in vain. There is meaning in everything, and PATIENCE is there to help you understand this.

You need to have PATIENCE with yourself and PATIENCE with others, then PATIENCE will open many doors, which otherwise might have remained closed. PATIENCE helps you see the bigger vision from a cosmic point of view. PATIENCE teaches you that you have an important part to play but that you need to trust and listen carefully to your refined intuition.

Those who have infinite PATIENCE experience infinite peace and are showered with many unexpected gifts.

SEED 24
FLOW

———

Life is like a river that FLOWS; it is a never ending journey with its twists and turns, opportunities, and unexpected occurrences. How you respond to life is up to you: you can respond to it with joy and gratitude or you can create obstacles and hold yourself back. Your attitude makes all the difference.

When you respond to life, you find you are in the FLOW: things come easily, they fall into place, they unfold one after another, and your desires are fulfilled without effort. However when you react to life, when you go against it and do not meet it willingly, you come up against yourself, you get in your own way, and nothing seems to work.

FLOW implies fluidity, movement, and change; it is the opposite of stagnation. Sometimes the FLOW is fast and strong, at other times there is less movement and patience is required. If you find yourself in a stagnant pool, where there is no FLOW and where nothing seems to be moving, then you need to examine closely and find out how you put yourself there and how you can move back into the mainstream and FLOW with life again.

FLOW and enjoy the journey. Let go of the attachment to the outcome. Enjoy the process, say yes to life, respond to life and it will respond to you.

Reflections on
FLOW

———

When you are in the FLOW, you are connected to the whole of life, and your heart opens up and the universe does everything to support you. If you feel disconnected and no longer feel within the FLOW of life, then somehow you have created this and you need to look and discover how and why.

An open heart says yes to life and receives support from everything around. When you FLOW with life, you are living in accordance with the laws of nature, and the higher realms will support you and bring people, circumstances, and opportunities to your door.

FLOW with the tide and allow it to carry you and release your burdens along the way. Be aware of how sweet life can taste, and have gratitude for all that which unfolds. Be in the FLOW and enjoy the riches that life has to offer; move with ease and give up all struggle and strain and see how quickly your life changes when you are in the FLOW.

SEED 25

OPENNESS

OPENNESS invites new things to come to you, new ideas and new ways of living your life. OPENNESS requires an OPEN heart that attracts people and invites a connection and communication. OPENNESS welcomes and extends, whereas fear closes doors and isolates.

OPENNESS enjoys being in the flow and works with ease and joy. When you are OPEN you come from a space of receptivity, which naturally attracts. OPENNESS appreciates change and knows the value of being flexible and patient. OPENNESS allows and goes with the flow and does not resist or limit or engage in judgement. OPENNESS dissolves barriers and limitations and continues to hold an expansive point of view.

When you are OPEN, there is never a dull moment, life is always exciting, and every day brings something new.

Reflections on
OPENNESS

———

OPENNESS will bestow upon you the bountiful gifts that life wishes to offer you. When you are in the flow of life, and you pay attention, you will see that something new is offered in every moment; but if you are not OPEN to what is there right in front of you, it may pass you by.

OPENNESS offers the opportunity for new people to walk into your life at any given moment, and with OPENNESS you never know what will present itself next. OPENNESS allows the unexpected to turn up on your doorstep. OPENNESS will always extend a helping hand, both for the giver and the receiver. OPENNESS appreciates and is full of gratitude, and recognizes the process of exchange.

OPENNESS invites you to dance with life, and to allow life to flow through you. So be OPEN to receive and enjoy the benefits and fruits of life.

SEED 26

SYNCHRONICITY

When you are open and awake and your mind is clear, you will notice more and more the SYNCHRONICITY that occurs in your life. SYNCHRONICITY takes place in the power of the present moment. You find yourself in the right place at the right time and subsequent events occur. The more in tune you are with the laws of nature, the more the natural laws will work with you and through you, bringing things together at the right moment and fulfilling your desires. When you are attuned to the realms of spirit and aware of the universal forces around you, you become conscious of how things work, and of the perfection of the universal laws that initiate SYNCHRONICITY.

As you observe SYNCHRONICITY at play within your life, you will be able to predict many things and to become a conscious co-creator with the universe. Then you will release any doubts, for your experiences will show you what is possible and a deep inner knowing will replace any worries or fears.

When SYNCHRONICITY occurs, you stand in awe and smile at the wonder of what is taking place. With SYNCHRONICITY, a deep gratitude develops for the universal gifts that are given to you and for the inexplicable way in which the cosmic forces can create and bring things together at any given time.

Watch the magic unfolding within your life and the SYNCHRO-NICITIES that occur at every step, but never take it for granted and always remember to give thanks.

Reflections on
SYNCHRONICITY

The more you are able to create a harmonious and peaceful state and to live your life from a place of stillness and beingness, the more you will see SYNCHRONICITY increasing in your life. When you are in the flow, things occur easily, without effort and the vibrations that you give out make the difference to what you receive. You have to come into alignment first within yourself and then with your surrounding environment and this will enable you to attract that which you desire and the universe will support you in your endeavours.

Punctuality is an important element in SYNCHRONICITY; make sure you are always on time. The universe is very precise in its alignments, being on time is an important part of your personal alignment with the cosmic pattern that unfolds your destiny. Those who have difficulty with being on time usually cannot manage their lives well and so they do not have peace of mind.

Reflect on the times that SYNCHRONICITY occurred in your life. As you become more conscious, SYNCHRONICITY can become a close friend and help you in countless ways. It is no coincidence who comes into your life or crosses your path; everything is divinely ordained according to the laws of karma but you have to be awake so as not to miss out on SYNCHRONICITY.

One never knows what might occur or when; this is part of the mystery of life. So choose to engage in a fruitful relationship with SYNCHRONICITY and create a purposeful dance with life.

SEED 27

REVIEW

———

This week take time to review the previous nine Seeds. Observe the thread that weaves between them and how well they work together and which ones need the most attention.

VIBRATION

CONTEMPLATION

FOCUS

INTENTION

FLEXIBILTY

PATIENCE

FLOW

OPENNESS

SYNCHRONICITY

REFLECTIONS

———

Reflect on the following affirmations, which are aligned to the previous nine Seeds.

I VIBRATE on a high level, which attracts similar VIBRATIONS to me.

I CONTEMPLATE my life deeply and therein find all the answers I need.

I hold one pointed FOCUS.

My INTENTIONS are clear.

I am FLEXIBLE and PATIENT.

I go with the FLOW and my life is easy and effortless.

I am OPEN to receive the gifts of the universe.

I am attuned with SYNCHRONICITY and easily draw the right people and circumstances that I need into my life. I am always in the right place at the right time.

SEED 28
FREEDOM

———

FREEDOM is an inner quality, which expresses itself through the way you live your life. FREEDOM is an inner state that comes from knowing who you are. FREEDOM allows you to live your life in the way that you choose and to feel FREE to make the choices that enhance your life and support your path of learning. FREEDOM cannot be restricted by outer conditioning or others' judgements, interferences, or limitations. FREEDOM encourages true expression of the heart and soul. True FREEDOM, once found, is something that no one can take away from you.

FREEDOM invites you to release the shackles of the past and to recognize when it is time to move on. Only you can give yourself the permission to be FREE.

FREEDOM allows you to follow your heart and to express yourself in your own unique way. FREEDOM offers you the choice to be open and to share or to be still and silent, according to how you feel in the moment. FREEDOM comes from a strength that develops from within, after having passed through certain life experiences that reveal the value of being true to yourself.

FREEDOM is the beacon which, once acknowledged, can shine so brightly in your life that it becomes the guiding light at the end of the tunnel.

Reflections on
FREEDOM

————

The more you are able to detach from emotional dramas and allow yourself to flow with life, the FREER you become. When you give up all thoughts of struggle and remain true to yourself, you can reach the highest fulfilment that you desire, as you become the observer watching your life unfolding beautifully with ease and calm.

When you do things that are not in alignment with your highest truth and deepest sense of knowing, you go against yourself; this blocks your way and restricts your FREEDOM. But when you learn to listen carefully to yourself, and closely follow the signs and your intuition, you will find the way to set yourself FREE. Then as you dare to be more courageous and live your life from the centre of your being in the way that you desire and know is right for you, you will discover a FREEDOM you had never anticipated.

Expressing yourself from your essence, from a state of inner FREEDOM, brings the ultimate joy. To do this you may need to move out of your comfort zone, or release relationships, either work related or personal, that are stagnant or joyless and do not fulfil your whole being. Such relationships confine and restrict and prevent you from exploring and actualizing your true purpose in being here. They are most often maintained because of the fear of letting go and what the unknown and unexpected might bring. Whereas FREEDOM cherishes the unexpected for it knows that anything is possible and there are no limitations other than those you impose upon yourself.

FREEDOM wants you to move forward in leaps and bounds, to fly as high as the sky, to explore the horizons, and to go even further beyond. FREEDOM encourages you to dream and be creative. If you wish to create a new reality, the life that you desire, you have to first set yourself FREE and transform any thought forms that are not in alignment with your highest vision and deepest sense of self. Don't let your life pass you by. Keep your vision and dreams passionately alive; don't let them fall by the wayside.

FREEDOM allows, FREEDOM is, FREEDOM opens you to a deeper level of wisdom and spontaneity that brings forth your creativity and full potential.

CREATIVITY

———

CREATIVITY is like a bubbling brook that flows forth with joy and enthusiasm and wants to keep flowing. Sometimes CREATIVITY bursts forth in a very strong and passionate way; at other times it is a gentle but steady flow. Occasionally CREATIVITY may be brought to a standstill, usually at times when you feel emotionally low or out of touch with yourself.

Your CREATIVITY is a reflection of your inner state. When you are in the flow and feeling open and free, you can CREATE abundantly, without effort; and the right people and circumstances will easily be drawn to you. CREATIVITY is similar to being in love, you feel a sense of oneness and you want to share and express yourself; it feels so joyful to be in the CREATIVE flow. When you are in this spirit, and CREATIVITY is flowing abundantly, everything seems attainable.

CREATIVITY is your *shakti* power, your potential to CREATE that is always there in unmanifest form, just waiting to be expressed. You can tap into the infinite reservoir of CREATIVITY at any given moment, and the Seeds are wonderful tools of transformation to help you discover everything that will help you do this.

The flow of CREATIVITY begins from an inner point of stillness, and as you allow yourself the freedom to be more open, your CREATIVITY will flow and flow abundantly. Do everything you can to encourage the dynamic free flow of your CREATIVITY and to remove any limitations that may impede your CREATIVE flow.

Explore and be CREATIVE like a child, remain in awe at the wonders of life. Let go of any disappointments. Don't brood on them; allow them to disappear quickly and replace them with the continual desire to CREATE, to explore and to develop your CREATIVITY in whatever way appeals to you, so that you can express and live your full potential in every possible way.

Reflections on
CREATIVITY

CREATIVITY is the spark that keeps your zest for life alive; it is always new; sometimes it is demanding but never boring. CREATIVITY takes you out of the mundane and into the realms of dreams, possibilities, and miracles.

You are the CREATOR of your life; you have to take full responsibility for everything that is happening. You are the artist, the painter, the architect, and the designer of your life. You wrote the script and you can rewrite it any time you desire, and you can do this again and again, as many times as you like. Your life can never be stagnant once you realize you have the power to CREATE.

Think about what you want to CREATE. Unleash your tremendous potential, allow your imagination to play, and let your CREATIVITY flow. You CREATE your life through your thoughts and your beliefs; so pay attention to the nature of your thoughts and what you constantly think about. Your life is a manifestation of your thoughts. CREATIVITY is the process of manifestation, of bringing the unmanifest into the world.

From a space of purity and openness, CREATIVITY flows. Within you lies a richness, depth, and deep knowing. CREATIVITY can bring forth your full potential and help you create a new blueprint for your life, which you can keep CREATING and RECREATING and redesigning as you desire.

As a CREATOR you need to be free to CREATE and do what you love to do. CREATIVITY is a conscious process of allowing, being with, and watching the unfoldment of CREATION. CREATIVITY also requires a clear mind, clear intentions, and dedicated focus.

SEED 30

ORGANIZATION

The universe knows how to ORGANIZE and bring things together. Nothing is by chance or at random: there is a higher plan for humanity in which we all have an important part to play. There are certain ORGANIZING principles constantly at work in the universe, trying to maintain the balance that is needed. The laws of nature ORGANIZE, create, construct, manifest, and hold, or transform, change, and deconstruct according to the needs of the time.

Everything is in constant motion, with ORGANIZATION at the central core. As individuals we are a reflection of the macrocosm and need to ORGANIZE our lives accordingly. ORGANIZATION is an important part of determining what you manifest in your life.

ORGANIZATION begins in the mind with clarity of thought and intention. A mind that is cluttered, unclear, or confused will have difficulty in manifesting. ORGANIZATION requires determination, stability, and energy. The clearer you are, the easier it becomes to understand the power of the ORGANIZING principles that are at work universally and in your own personal life. This then enables you to work with these principles rather than against them. The more you live your life in tune with the laws of nature, and the more ORGANIZED you are, the easier things will fall into place as you flow effortlessly with life.

ORGANIZATION is the ability to prepare well, to plan, and stay focused on your intent but to also have the flexibility to change and restructure where necessary. ORGANIZATION requires patience; it may take time to bring things together. ORGANIZATION is a step by step process of creation, unfoldment, and manifestation, which can be continuously modified and improved according to the needs of the moment.

Reflections on
ORGANIZATION

Paying attention to becoming more ORGANIZED in your life is essential and this works on many levels. Disorganization brings discomfort. When you are well ORGANIZED, you feel more at peace within yourself and create harmony in your environment. Feng Shui, Vaastu, and Sacred Geometry are examples of universal principles that use ORGANIZATION as a key to bringing about harmony, tranquillity, and synchronization.

All manifestation requires ORGANIZATION in some way in order to bring the pieces or parts together in the right way at the right time. Time is an important element in ORGANIZATION; time requires that you calculate and prepare well so you can create a schedule that allows certain activities to be fulfilled.

As you become more ORGANIZED in your mind and there is more synthesis between the left and right brain, this will affect every area of your life and spread out further afield to your environment and continue to draw to you whatever you need. Never allow yourself to sabotage that which you are intending; maintain your focus on becoming more ORGANIZED and you will reap the benefits that will become evident in every area of your life.

SEED 31
EMPOWERMENT

———

Real EMPOWERMENT comes from deep within, from a place of knowing within oneself. Spiritual practices such as meditation and self reflection lead you to EMPOWERMENT. The more you know yourself, the closer you come to being able to express and live your truth without fear; this is true EMPOWERMENT.

EMPOWERMENT does not falter in the face of adversity: it faces challenges with courage. EMPOWERED by your inner strength, you have the confidence to carry on and to take things in your stride, knowing that your consistency will eventually help you to attain what you desire.

EMPOWERMENT is about taking full responsibility for your life and what you create. EMPOWERMENT is being able to stand firmly in your own power and to make the right decisions for yourself. EMPOWERMENT asks you to look at any emotional patterns that are still active within your life and interfere with your process of becoming fully EMPOWERED. EMPOWERMENT impels you to take active, practical steps to achieve your desires and to banish all lethargy, laziness, and procrastination.

EMPOWERMENT and organization walk hand in hand. Through creating a greater vision for your life, you realize the need for organization to bring all the pieces together in the most creative way. EMPOWERMENT gives you the faith, trust, and assurance that you have the ability to succeed in whatever you choose to do.

Reflections on
EMPOWERMENT

——

When you speak your truth from the highest level of integrity, you will feel incredibly EMPOWERED. As you move from being disempowered to being EMPOWERED, your life will change dramatically. It will be as if you have taken a quantum leap and suddenly find yourself on the other side of life, where you have always wanted to be.

EMPOWERMENT encourages you to live by your own principles and values, and not to be affected by the opinions of others nor to just follow the crowd. EMPOWERED people are individuals who follow their own unique path and consequently feel fulfilled and look forward to every day with joy. EMPOWERMENT invites you to come out of hiding, to become more visible and not to be afraid to take the next step that life presents to you. EMPOWERMENT encourages you to live your life with passion and joy, to do what you love to do, and to follow your refined intuition at all times.

There is a whole world out there just waiting to be explored, but you have to open up to it and take the necessary steps. EMPOWERMENT will help you go out there and embrace everything your heart and soul desire. When you are spiritually EMPOWERED, you can literally feel spirit moving through every area of your life, you know you are in the flow, and nothing can hold you back. Now is the time to EMPOWER yourself, to move forward and to take a quantum leap.

SEED 32

ABUNDANCE

We live in an ABUNDANT universe, where everything you can ever dream of is already there in unmanifest form just waiting to be manifested. When you hold the consciousness of ABUNDANCE everything comes to you easily.

ABUNDANCE asks that you release all limiting patterns that keep you in lack of any kind. Old patterns of lack or limitation need to be transformed into a consciousness of ABUNDANCE. Lack and ABUNDANCE are two sides of the same coin: which one will you choose? Empowerment points you in the direction of ABUNDANCE and refuses to allow you to get drawn back into the limitations of the past, but instead offers you a new way forward to total ABUNDANCE on every level.

ABUNDANCE offers you a whole new way of seeing and living; it invites you through vision and empowerment to live an ABUNDANT life. When your mind and consciousness are focused clearly on ABUNDANCE and you do not allow anything to interfere or sabotage your intentions, then with patience and a clear vision, your expectations will no doubt be fulfilled. Through being open and finding the freedom within yourself that allows you to move effortlessly into the flow of life, ABUNDANCE will draw to you all that you need and much more.

ABUNDANCE is about living a life that is rich and prosperous in every possible way. ABUNDANCE is not just about money, it is about creating a life that is rich, fulfilling and rewarding. ABUNDANCE asks you to be truly generous and to offer your services and to share whatever you have with others. Generosity of spirit does not entertain selfishness, holding, or hoarding, instead it encourages sharing so you can keep the energy flowing by embodying the principle that the more you give the more you will receive. ABUNDANCE does not entertain scarcity or any limiting thought forms; instead ABUNDANCE chooses expansiveness, limitlessness, vastness, and depth.

ABUNDANCE is always attuned to the limitless supply of the universe, whose doors are always open to those who are aligned with a higher perspective and understand the principles of giving and receiving.

Reflections on
ABUNDANCE

———

Generosity begins at home and from there ABUNDANCE starts and spreads. Home is within you; ABUNDANCE and prosperity start from your inner being. You have to feel ABUNDANT to embrace ABUNDANCE, and then you can give out ABUNDANCE. Whatever you give out, you will receive back in ABUNDANT amounts. The underlying principles of ABUNDANCE require the understanding of the karmic relationship between giving and receiving, and the awareness of what you sow, so shall you reap.

ABUNDANCE requires the openness of a generous heart and deep gratitude for everything that has and is being given. ABUNDANCE is about the exchange of energy, of manifesting creative ideas and joyful ways of living, and fulfilling your potential and life purpose, so you can experience and share the greatest joy.

ABUNDANCE needs the constant planting of new Seeds, watching their germination, caring for them, and nurturing them on a daily basis. You cannot plant the Seeds and then ignore them, for they will wither and die. If you want your Seeds of ABUNDANCE to sprout, flourish, and bring forth a rich harvest, then you have to nurture them well on a daily basis.

ABUNDANCE is yours when you desire to claim it. Make sure you choose the right side of the coin.

MANIFESTATION

MANIFESTATION is the process of being able to bring whatever you deeply desire into the physical reality. MANIFESTATION includes the ability to visualize clearly your desired intention and to continue to focus on it until it reaches the point of MANIFESTATION. Many people give up on their projects far too early; they don't have the patience or the staying power that is required for MANIFESTATION to occur.

MANIFESTATION needs an unlimited mind that can hold an expansive point of view and see many possibilities. It also needs flexibility, depth, passion, and a commitment to what you believe in. When your thinking is clear and you do not allow anything to cloud your vision, then MANIFESTATION occurs more easily and you see the steps you need to take for the realization of your vision.

Sitting quietly in a peaceful relaxed state and taking your desired outcome into meditation can greatly assist the process of MANIFESTATION. All of the Seeds that you have worked with until now have paved the way towards MANIFESTATION. Each one has an important part to play and shows you your strengths and weaknesses. Any weak link in the chain may interfere with the MANIFESTATION of what you desire.

Clearing your consciousness of all limiting thoughts and old patterns that no longer serve you are necessary steps for MANIFESTATION so that you can access and MANIFEST your dreams and make them your reality. It takes work; you need to be constantly alert and pay attention, and no one else is going to do it for you, so you have to remain strongly committed to your own process of MANIFESTATION. You have the tools to work with, the Seeds, those that have already been given and those that are yet to follow.

See yourself as an alchemist at work, clear and focused on the task at hand, using your creativity and unlimited potential as you observe the unfoldment of your chosen MANIFESTATION.

Reflections on
MANIFESTATION

As you keep your attention positively on what you wish to MANIFEST, the plentiful universe will provide. Abundance and support will come to you. Be consistent in what you wish to achieve and do not allow any contradictions to sabotage your efforts. Make sure you do not have any conflicting patterns running at the same time, which could interfere with your MANIFESTATION. Ask for assistance when you need it, both from your support team on the physical realm as well as from those on the higher planes who are always waiting to assist.

As you learn how to MANIFEST more effectively through practice and gradually increasing your expertise, you will recognize spirit moving though your life, guiding and assisting in many ways. Suddenly doors that were closed will open and new people may come into your life that will help you MANIFEST your vision. Likewise old friends may reappear and be there to support you. Expect the unexpected, be open, trust the process, and relax into it.

Hold the greatest possible vision for your life, and keep working, expanding and refining it every day. By doing this, you will see how you can MANIFEST your dreams and visions and continue to MANIFEST in every area of your life in new and rewarding ways.

Spiritual empowerment is about having a great vision and having the ability to MANIFEST that vision. Take a bird's eye view and see the pieces of the puzzle coming together, look for any missing or weak links, repair them and move on. Don't allow any limitations or old programming from the past to hold you back, let your creative ideas flow freely, and remember there are no limitations other than those you create and impose upon yourself. Become a master of MANIFESTATION.

SEED 34
INTEGRITY

Living your life with INTEGRITY will help eliminate certain patterns and trends from your consciousness that are not in alignment with the deeper truth of who you really are. INTEGRITY encourages you to constantly improve yourself and raise your consciousness. INTEGRITY reminds you to do unto others as you would have them do unto you and to include it as a code that you live your life by. When you treat people with INTEGRITY, they will treat you in the same way. Put yourself in the other person's shoes to see how it feels and this will help you to have more compassion and kindness. Seeing where people are and the difficulties they face helps avoid judgement. Don't judge others or gossip; instead get on with your own business and pay attention to improving yourself.

INTEGRITY asks you to be just and fair, and to keep your word and not to make promises you cannot fulfil. Don't blame when things don't appear to be going the way you wish; instead look deep within yourself to find out why. Always use self reflection to find your answers. Instead of projecting, look within yourself to see how you can improve a situation. When in doubt wait, be patient, and ask for assistance from the higher realms or find someone to work with who will help you move through your limitations. The more you consider others and relinquish selfishness, the more you will find appreciation and understanding coming your way.

INTEGRITY reminds you to be as sincere and honest as you can, to speak your truth when it is needed and to remain silent when discernment indicates that this is the wisest thing to do. Always choose your words carefully; the way you express yourself can make all the difference. Try to maintain a high level of INTEGRITY in everything you say and do. Be impeccable in your interactions with everyone. Impeccable actions reap great benefits and balance the karmic scales in your favour.

Reflections on
INTEGRITY

Real INTEGRITY begins with respect. Respecting others begins with self respect. If you do not treat yourself with INTEGRITY and respect, you will not receive it from anyone else. Respect yourself, your fellow human beings, and the planet. Have a deep consideration of others and listen carefully. Be a responsible citizen and help create a better world through working with INTEGRITY. Don't be passive or just follow the crowd; listen to your intuition carefully about what is right for you, follow your own truth and take action, and in this way you can make a difference in your own life and positively affect the lives of those around you.

INTEGRITY demands genuineness: you cannot say one thing and do another. Determine to strengthen any weak areas in your character by working on the Seeds of Transformation again and again until you iron out any imperfections. Use INTEGRITY to expand your consciousness and to give you the insights you require to live a fulfilling, wonderful, and abundant life.

SEED 35
GRATITUDE

GRATITUDE implies a humbleness of spirit, of acknowledging and being thankful for something that is happening in your life or to those around you. Being GRATEFUL on a daily basis can completely change your life. If you remember to be GRATEFUL for every gift and opportunity that comes your way, you will find yourself being showered with many blessings. Giving and receiving walk hand in hand, so take every opportunity to show your GRATITUDE.

When you bring GRATITUDE into your life, you will never again experience a dull moment, and depression and despondency will never be able to take a foothold in your life again. Everywhere you look, you can find something to be GRATEFUL for. GRATITUDE will increase your feeling of abundance and as you share it, you will attract more of the same.

Give blessings, share blessings, and be GRATEFUL for everything that is happening. Smile at life and it will smile back at you. Open your heart in GRATITUDE and watch miracles occur.

GRATITUDE develops an aura of grace, which encompasses thanksgiving, appreciation, and an acceptance of what is in the moment. GRATITUDE is a gift you can give abundantly to everyone and it will transform your relationships.

Reflections on
GRATITUDE
—

Be GRATEFUL for every desire that is fulfilled, for every manifestation that occurs. Be GRATEFUL for the opportunities that life presents, for the lessons learnt, and for the chance to try again and make amends. Be GRATEFUL for every meeting and every person you encounter, for every smile you receive, unexpected connection, or time spent with a friend. Be GRATEFUL for times of solace and reflection as well as activity and recreation. Be GRATEFUL for every new person that comes into your life.

Be GRATEFUL for the abundance and joy that nature gives, the changing of the different seasons, the variety of different terrains, the waxing and waning of the moon, and the glorious sunlight that warms and heals. Be GRATEFUL for every special moment and know that nothing is in vain; everything has purpose and meaning, even if you cannot yet see or understand it.

Life itself is a miracle. Give GRATITUDE for being here and endeavour to appreciate every day. GRATITUDE is like a flower that opens and blossoms and radiates its inner beauty. Be GRATEFUL and allow yourself to unfold within the spirit of GRATITUDE. Don't let any day pass by without showing GRATITUDE, it is the simplest of gifts, yet it can bring the greatest of rewards.

Be GRATEFUL for everything that is happening, including the development of your spiritual progress and the chosen way you have designed to follow. Never go to sleep at night without saying thank you for what has occurred during the day. Be GRATEFUL for the dawn of the next day and what it might possibly bring and determine to make it special.

SEED 36
FORGIVENESS

FORGIVENESS is the key to happiness; it opens the door to love and sets the soul free. FORGIVENESS stirs the heart and purifies the consciousness. FORGIVENESS lifts the veils and releases you from the bindings of the past and softens even the hardest of hearts. One who cannot FORGIVE will never know what it means to be truly free. The more you work with gratitude, the more you will understand the necessity of FORGIVENESS.

FORGIVENESS releases the past, clears unfinished business, and offers a way for further clearing so you are able to move on. If you feel stuck in any area of your life, if things still don't seem to flow, then there is stagnant energy, which needs to be unblocked and moved; FORGIVENESS is the way to get it moving.

Begin with FORGIVING yourself by releasing any judgement or doubts about yourself and your actions of the past. The past has gone, but the present is here now. FORGIVE yourself and determine to move on and to make the best of every situation.

Look deeply into your heart and see who you still need to FORGIVE. Allow them the release, set them free and release any unforgiving energy that still binds you to them. In this way, you can free yourself to move onto the next level of experience that awaits you. Don't allow a lack of FORGIVENESS to be a stumbling block on your path towards enlightenment.

Reflections on
FORGIVENESS

A FORGIVING or unforgiving mind is only a viewpoint, one looks from one side whilst the other looks from the opposite. The unforgiving mind judges and attacks because it is full of fear and anger. It thinks it is justified in its point of view. An unforgiving mind cannot see and needs compassion, whereas a FORGIVING mind is compassionate, tolerant, and kind.

You are never upset for the reason you think, it is always a combination of many things, sitting layer upon layer upon your heart. If you don't clear and release, it will fester and prevent your own healing. When there is a resistance to FORGIVENESS, it is sad because there can be no release from pain and no room for love to come in. Holding resentment, anger, and pain keeps the doors of the heart closed and prevents wounds from being healed.

You cannot discern what is best for another or how they should behave. At the end of the day it is only yourself that you can look to and that is why FORGIVENESS starts with you; so FORGIVE yourself. If things are not working out in your life in the way that you want, look carefully to see what still weighs on your heart, be kind and compassionate with yourself and don't attack, blame, or accuse others. Instead, become more understanding and FORGIVING. You will feel a huge weight lift from your heart.

Don't waste your time or energy on trivial things that are not important or not truly meaningful for your life. FORGIVE, be charitable, and open your heart to allow the light in, then your whole perspective on life will change. When you FORGIVE, your footsteps will tread more lightly on the path and you will sleep more soundly. Slay the dragons of the past, FORGIVE, clear your conscience, and sleep with the angels.

SEED 37

COMPASSION

COMPASSION is the language of the heart that has been gained by a conscious traveller of life whilst passing through certain life experiences. Only an open heart that has developed enough emotional maturity can develop full COMPASSION. COMPASSION looks deeply and realizes that nothing is as it seems. Behind every story is another story, eventually tracing back through the journey of lifetimes.

COMPASSION does not search vainly for answers; it just remains open, allows, and does not judge. You never know how much someone is suffering or what their circumstances are or how they can cope or deal with life.

COMPASSION sparks a desire to help or to be of service in whatever way is called for. COMPASSION engenders simple acts of kindness and acknowledges the person and is fully present with them in the moment. Being present with someone sparks a spiritual connection that is felt and understood, even if no words are even spoken between them.

COMPASSION empathizes and holds the person in light, peace, and love. COMPASSION is a genuine exchange from one heart to another. COMPASSION gives generously but expects nothing in return.

Reflections on
COMPASSION

COMPASSION is a wonderful gift to give to each other; most times it happens spontaneously because it is simply felt in the moment. With COMPASSION, the heart opens and loving energy pours forth. Although COMPASSION sympathizes, it knows how to support without getting drawn into dramas. COMPASSION is considerate, caring, and patient; it goes with the flow of what is unfolding and remains steady, holding an unwavering gaze. At the same time, COMPASSION knows how to use discernment and remain detached when necessary.

It is through COMPASSION that a person can achieve the highest peak in his or her search for self fulfilment, because COMPASSION also embraces unconditional love. COMPASSION is a very important stepping stone for those who wish to move in the direction of enlightenment. COMPASSION invites you to look in the mirror and to understand what you see. What is reflected back to you is what you need to acknowledge. Be gentle on yourself and treat yourself with COMPASSION and once you have really embraced and embodied it, then COMPASSION will be one of the greatest gifts that you can give.

SEED 38
COMMUNICATION

Good COMMUNICATION is necessary in every walk of life. No matter what your work or circumstances, clear, precise COMMUNICATION is essential. Relationships are based on COMMUNICATION: the more authentic and honest the COMMUNICATION, the clearer the level of exchange and interaction.

COMMUNICATION is the unspoken language of the heart. When people COMMUNICATE only from the level of the head and not the heart, there is no real meeting, no deep connection, and eventually that COMMUNICATION may break down or dry up, whereas heart COMMUNICATION demands respect and integrity and it builds friendships that can last forever. COMMUNICATION also takes place without words; our body language and actions speak for themselves. Most relationships, whether personal or business, break down because of misunderstandings created through a lack of proper COMMUNICATION.

COMMUNICATION breaks down barriers; it helps to maintain and create new relationships. It opens doors, it is the way in, and it starts a flow that keeps things moving. Leaders in all fields are good COMMUNICATORS. Those who hold back and do not COMMUNICATE their thoughts, feelings, or ideas tend to get left out or be ignored. COMMUNICATION is an energetic exchange between people: it extends, shares, and welcomes, and when expressed in the right spirit is always appreciated.

Reflections on
COMMUNICATION

The most important person you need to COMMUNICATE with is yourself; and it is especially important to be honest with yourself about what is working for you and what is not. Your refined intuition will tell you what you need to know and what you need to do. Meditation is a way of COMMUNING with yourself. When you connect on a daily basis with your innermost wisdom, the answers will come. This daily COMMUNION with yourself is the most precious time of the day; don't neglect it.

As you let go of fear and learn to COMMUNICATE your needs, you will find yourself contributing more to life and then life will in some way give something special back to you. Self expression keeps the flow of COMMUNICATION going and then in turn the feedback you receive makes you feel valued and appreciated. COMMUNICATION is a two way process, but you have to understand that not everyone COMMUNICATES in the same way, so their way may be different from yours.

The development of good listening skills is an important part of COMMUNICATION; a person knows when they are really being seen and heard. Sharing, participating, networking, and brainstorming are all important parts of the COMMUNICATION process. When you are authentic in your COMMUNICATION, when you are speaking, expressing, and living your truth, it feels right, and the other person feels it too.

There are many ways to contribute and be of service, but all of them can be enhanced through good COMMUNICATION skills. Relationships need nurturing, and open and honest COMMUNICATION is important in every relationship. An idea that has not been expressed just withers and is forgotten; the same can happen with a relationship. COMMUNICATION keeps ideas and relationships alive and flourishing.

Become an excellent communicator. Express your truth and share your light in everything you say and do.

SEED 39
HEALING

HEALING is a vast subject, and tomes of information have been written about it. HEALING implies a need for change; this could be on a physical, mental, emotional, or energetic level. Often where there is an energy block, it is because something from the past still needs to be released or an emotional wound or trauma needs to be HEALED.

HEALING can take place in whatever way is needed. Deep wounds may need a HEALING balm and the greatest balm is love. Listen to what you feel, don't suppress or ignore it. Where there is discomfort, look for the right sort of support that will nourish you in the way that you need.

HEALING unwinds, unlocks, and transforms and it brings release that sets you free from the past. What in you still needs HEALING or attention? At times we all need assistance, guidance, and support. When you feel there is a need for deeper HEALING, find someone to work with who will help you clear the cobwebs of the past so you can fully embrace the present and welcome the future. Only the past holds you back. Ask for the right person to come into your life and someone will appear.

Wild animals retreat, fast, and sleep when they need to HEAL. Most humans have forgotten how to turn inwards when HEALING is needed and have forgotten about the importance of relaxing, resting, and being quiet. Times of solitude and meditation are essential for any type of HEALING.

Time can also be a great HEALER; time helps you to see things differently, to forgive, have compassion, and to let go. HEALING starts in the mind, by the way you look at things and by changing your perception. Ask to see things differently, to gain more clarity and a new perspective that will assist you in your HEALING process.

Sometimes there are still lessons to be learnt, which take time; then HEALING cannot be achieved until this has been accomplished or until a shift in consciousness occurs or a deeper understanding is acquired.

Reflections on
HEALING
———

HEALING takes you to a new level where you can embrace love, warmth, kindness, tenderness, sweetness, and joy. HEALING replaces all fear and asks you to trust in the ultimate support of the divine. HEALING calls upon humility, forgiveness, and compassion to play an active role in the process of letting go.

HEALING acknowledges a higher power, the magnitude of which is difficult to imagine. HEALING calls upon the violet flame to purify and HEAL all karma and the crystalline Christ energy to HEAL through opening the door to love.

The spiral HEALING waves can cleanse and purify and remove the dross, including personal limitations and lower vibrations. HEALING waves can touch the soul and awaken the sleeping consciousness and lift you up to the transcendental realms, where purity and unity prevail.

Bring yourself back to balance, nurture yourself well. HEAL your mind, heart, and body all the way down to the cellular level. Clear out the remnants from the past, shed the skeins that have bound you so tightly, and set yourself free to take a new path, which will assist you on every level of your HEALING process.

Come to know who you are and appreciate your own personal journey of HEALING and everything you have encountered and learnt along the way, which has brought you to this amazing moment in time. Then as you move forward, you will feel free to explore the path that lies before you with gratitude and without fear. Then as a greater sense of self emerges, you can move from individual HEALING and begin to explore a whole other level of global HEALING wherein you can be of great service to humanity.

SEED 40
INTEGRATION

———

Now once again we take the time to pause and reflect and to INTEGRATE the previous Seeds that you have been working with before continuing with the last part of the course. As you reflect, you will see how things have come together and the influence and benefits of the work that you have done so far. You will also have gained insights into where your strengths and weaknesses lie and although you know there is more work to be done, you can also acknowledge that you are well on the way in your process of transformation.

The Seeds of Transformation have been planted in your consciousness, but they require continuous attention. The Seeds need to be nurtured and cared for and worked with again and again, as you continue with your ongoing cycle of personal growth and evolution.

INTEGRATION time is always helpful: it gives you the breathing space to stand back and see more clearly, to incorporate and assimilate, and it prepares you for that which is yet to come.

INTEGRATION allows you to recognize how far you have come, and to observe the unfolding of what is now taking place. INTEGRATION shows you that you have the ability to master the tools that have been given, so that you can attain whatever you wish to achieve in your life and lead a purposeful life propelled by the knowledge that you have gained so far.

REFLECTIONS

———

During the next week, take the time to reflect on the following Seeds and see which ones still need the most attention.

FREEDOM

CREATIVITY

ORGANIZATION

EMPOWERMENT

ABUNDANCE

MANIFESTATION

INTEGRITY

GRATITUDE

FORGIVENESS

COMPASSION

COMMUNICATION

HEALING

INTEGRATION

SEED 41

BALANCE

To maintain good health and a sense of well-being, you have to stay well BALANCED. You need to be clear about your priorities and what is important to you and what makes you feel good. Keeping the scales BALANCED is an important task that requires continuous attention as things are always changing, and this is the ever evolving nature of life.

The foundation of maintaining your BALANCE lies in centredness, peace, and serenity and having the willpower to stay on track and not losing your sense of direction or deviating from that which you know to be right for you. This needs a clear focus and if you are not well BALANCED, it is easy to lose your focus.

We live in a fast moving world, where many demands are put upon us. It takes discipline and determination to hold your BALANCE; but when you learn how to remain well BALANCED regardless of your outer circumstances, then you will be able to cope with whatever life brings and easily integrate and benefit from it.

BALANCE incorporates the yin and yang principles, the masculine and the feminine, and the active cooperation of the left and right sides of the brain, giving and receiving, and invoking and expressing. The task then is how to be attentive enough so that you are able to continue to maintain your BALANCE on a daily basis.

Meditation helps you to see more clearly what is happening and to develop a stronger sense of self, which keeps you centred and in BALANCE. It also helps you to become clearer from moment to moment on how to maintain this BALANCE.

Reflections on
BALANCE

———

Healing is about bringing yourself back to BALANCE. Imbalances and disease are created through a state of disharmony, which is often fed by fear. If your life is out of BALANCE, and you are feeling a lot of tension, stress, and strain, it is because you have allowed yourself to be pulled too far in one direction, and this has created an imbalance. Everything in you calls to REBALANCE so that you can re-establish your harmony and stability again. If you don't pay attention to what is happening and listen to the messages that your bodymind is giving you, and you go too far out of BALANCE, there may be consequences to pay.

Everything in life requires BALANCE; it is one of the universal laws. There needs to be BALANCE between activity and rest, work and play, inner and outer work, and between dynamic creativity and quiet, reflective time. Too much of anything can create an imbalance. There also needs to be a BALANCE between the material aspects of life and the spiritual; both need equal attention. We are spiritual beings living in a material world and we need to understand the importance of both and how they support and interact with each other, and that neither one can be neglected nor ignored

When there is BALANCE, life becomes an interesting interaction of different dynamics, with the individual acting as an observer at the centre of their own universe, consciously creating and manifesting. BALANCE responds by helping to maintain your creative flow and bringing forth your creative manifestations.

SEED 42
ALIGNMENT

What you are ALIGNED or attuned to is where your energy and attention are, and consequently this is what you draw to yourself. A spiritual ALIGNMENT is a connection to a higher power that supports and guides you, and according to your belief system this could be God, the Divine Presence, the ascended masters, or angelic beings.

ALIGNMENT needs balance. If you are off balance, you will not be properly ALIGNED with your intention or desires and may have difficulty manifesting. To ALIGN is to be in tune and to feel the free flow of energy, then things fall naturally into place without effort and the so called coincidences happen more often. When you are ALIGNED, you feel connected to something far greater than yourself and you know that you play an important part in the greater scheme of things.

There are different ways of ALIGNING: inner ALIGNMENT, postural and chakra ALIGNMENT, auric ALIGNMENT, environmental ALIGNMENT, planetary and cosmic ALIGNMENT.

Inner ALIGNMENT is when you are comfortable within yourself; then your whole being responds, allows, and feels attuned. You are aware of your chosen course, your life purpose, and watch it unfolding step by step. When this is the case, there is no need for impatience, for you know without a shadow of a doubt that as a co-creator you are in the right place at the right time and things happen exactly as they are meant to.

When you are ALIGNED within yourself, you see life as an exciting journey, and day by day your clarity of vision increases, revealing the next steps including the lessons to be learnt. Just as Seeds need to have their roots grounded in the earth, so you have to be grounded in your spirituality, and bring in the powerful, angelic energies and ground them in practical ways in your life. When this occurs, you find all your needs being taken care of and that the universe continuously opens the way and brings to you whatever is needed. Assistance is always given but you have to ALIGN and ask for what you need.

Reflections on
ALIGNMENT

You have to get clear on what you wish to ALIGN with and then practise holding your focus. Don't float through life or just be carried along with the crowd or the trends; instead choose purposeful and conscious living every single day of your life.

There are many directions you can choose to go but at the end of the day, it is your choice. What manifests in your life is the result of your choices. Use empowerment and discernment to make the decisions that are in ALIGNMENT with what you really want and then be totally committed. Remain open and flexible. Things change, you never know what tomorrow may bring or what new opportunities may be presented. Be willing to keep making adjustments when necessary. The more flexible you are, the easier it is to stay in the flow and ride with the ups and downs that life sometimes brings.

We are also affected by the gravitational effects of the planets and the cycles of the moon and this needs to also be taken into consideration. Sometimes your inner or environmental ALIGNMENT may be affected by certain constellations of the stars or by environmental catastrophes such as earthquakes and tidal waves. The earth needs time to make her own REALIGNMENTS and this affects everyone on the planet.

Sacred Geometry, Feng Shui, and Vaastu are systems that use ALIGNMENT as a way of improving and balancing your environmental ALIGNMENT. More advanced levels of this work also take into consideration planetary, universal, and cosmic ALIGNMENTS.

There are many doors waiting to be opened; practising conscious ALIGNMENT will bring you a deeper understanding that will give you the keys to opening those doors.

Always seek to ALIGN with the highest and deepest wisdom and with the truth that resonates within you and then you will always be divinely guided and inspired.

SEED 43

LIGHT

———

There is a universal source of LIGHT that permeates the entire universe and whether you are conscious of it or not, your inner being is always seeking an alignment to the LIGHT. Working with the LIGHT raises your spiritual vibration and changes your whole vibratory structure, thus allowing deeper healing to occur. According to the amount of LIGHT that an individual is able to draw in and hold, this influences how much time and energy is needed for transformation to occur. This also depends on the consciousness of the person and the preparatory work that has been done.

The embodiment of LIGHT is a gradual process. At first the LIGHT that is drawn in has to penetrate through many dense layers before it can reach down to the cellular level. When the LIGHT clears the dross and reaches the cellular level, the DNA can be influenced and hereditary and karmic patterns can shift and be transformed.

The LIGHT paves the way as it clears illusions and discards denser energies and limiting patterns. The LIGHT cuts through and shines upon the truth. When the LIGHT begins to shine in your consciousness, you become a magnet that attracts everything that is good and pure to you to assist you on your journey towards enlightenment. A LIGHT filled body has lifted its awareness to a higher level and radiates vibrations of harmony, peace, bliss, and love.

Reflections on
LIGHT

Working with the LIGHT is a constant challenge; it involves staying conscious all the time. It requires living a life of high integrity and trusting in what is happening in the moment, even if the way does not yet seem clear. You can utilize the LIGHT for all your consciousness and healing work; it is there to be used and drawn upon. The higher realms will assist you in whatever way is needed if you are continuously aligned with them. Those who wish to be of service will be opened to the LIGHT when they are ready.

There is always more work to be done; the LIGHT will guide you. Being in the LIGHT reveals the true reality of things as the veils are drawn aside. The energies of the Christ consciousness will continually lift you up as you move more and more into the fullness of the LIGHT and allow it to fill your whole being.

The more you expand and share your LIGHT with everyone you encounter, the more it is reflected back to you. Then you become a shining LIGHT that acts as a beacon for those in need to find you. This is the way of the LIGHTWORKER'S path, but first you need to fully embrace the LIGHT and transform yourself. The intentions you hold change as you become LIGHTER and you allow the LIGHT to shine upon your every step.

As your consciousness expands, it will connect to the cosmic levels, and you will be drawn to other LIGHT beings around the world. Then you will be able to blend your LIGHT with other LIGHTWORKERS so you can help each other create a beautiful web of LIGHT around the planet. As a LIGHTWORKER, you will discover that this is one of your main purposes in being here, to spread the LIGHT and take the LIGHT out into the world. Then every step of your journey will be truly blessed.

SEED 44
TRUST

There is nothing more powerful than TRUSTING that your life is divinely guided and that cosmic beings walk with you, preparing the way. At the beginning of your spiritual journey, it takes a lot of TRUST to believe this and to clear out the negative and limiting thought patterns that still pervade your consciousness. Walking the path of truth is empowered by a deep knowing, which comes gradually through experience.

Once you have felt the angelic wings enfolding you with love and compassion or been given glimpses of something that you know is beyond your own level of creation, then the tide turns and you start to TRUST that you are connected and guided by an all pervading, Divine Presence. When this happens, there is no going back and doubt becomes impossible.

Those experiential moments that open you to the cosmic realms, and on occasion grant you extraordinary transcendental experiences, can dramatically change your life and dissolve the doubts and fears. Such experiences register in your consciousness and lead to the building of TRUST until you reach a point when you no longer need to question, because you just know. When intention and certainty meet, TRUST emerges.

The light of truth brings freedom and an inner security. This inner security by far surpasses any outer security, which will always be limited. TRUST will encourage you to move forward to explore a limitless world with infinite possibilities.

Reflections on
TRUST

———

Surrender all of your fears, anxieties, doubts, and regrets to a higher power and TRUST that they will be resolved. As you further empower yourself to clear away the distorted illusions of life, you will find yourself in alignment with the Divine Presence.

According to what colour tinted glasses you are wearing determines how you see the world. The world is safe when you decide it is safe, it is supportive and loving when you feel it is so. Let TRUST be the guiding force that now enters your life and don't lose your TRUST even on the most difficult of days. Surrender all fearful thoughts, attachments, and belief systems that you have been holding onto which no longer serve you.

TRUST that you know what is right for you and can make the right decisions for your life, guided by your refined intuition, and that when extra support and guidance are needed, you will find them. TRUST that in all circumstances the truth will be revealed to you. TRUST leads to the freedom to live your life in the way you desire, without limitations.

Make TRUST the foundation from where you live your life and let the universe take care of the details.

SEED 45
JOY

JOY is like a bubbling brook within you; it just bubbles up and spills over and replenishes those around you. JOY is contagious. When you are full of JOY, it is so easy to share it. People look everywhere to find happiness, but you just have to be still and look inside. You may need to clear away a few layers to reach it, but JOY is there waiting patiently to be found.

The more you learn to trust and follow your intuition and the callings of your heart, the closer you will come to JOY. Don't get stuck in your limitations, look at your potential and the possibilities that lie before you. Discover what brings you JOY and bring more of it into your life. Begin and end the day with JOY and always give thanks. ENJOY every precious moment, savour everything that gives you pleasure, and be deeply grateful for whatever touches your heart and brings you JOY. Remember those JOYFUL times, register the feelings, and let the rest go. Release, forgive, and move on and choose to stay with JOY instead.

It is the simple things in life that bring the greatest JOY and most often they are free; like a stroll in nature, quiet peaceful moments, or special times shared with a friend. The good things in life may not be the most obvious, and material wealth may make life more comfortable but real wealth is found elsewhere. It is the gifts of the spirit, which have the greatest meaning, that bring the ultimate JOY. Where there is inner beauty and depth and an appreciation of the simplicity and JOY of life, then your whole being will respond with JOY; it just bubbles up from inside.

JOY is a state of being: when it is released and allowed its freedom, it will express itself abundantly.

Reflections on
JOY

Putting your life on course so that you become aligned with your life purpose will bring you JOY. Do things that increase your JOY and avoid situations and people that drain your energy or don't make you happy. Don't be afraid to take risks when the situation calls for it. If you follow your intuition and act accordingly, you will magnetize that which brings you the greatest JOY. So follow your intuition in what feels right for you.

Believe in yourself and your ability to create a JOY filled life. Trust the process and draw JOY to you by engaging passionately in the exploration of life. Find the JOY that is always there but may be hidden by unfinished business from the past. Feel the JOY of the moment. Don't let the past get in the way, embrace the sweetness of life, and live it to the full.

Fill every cell of your body with JOY; ENJOY lightness of heart and be carefree in spirit. Feel the bubbles of JOY that wish to burst forth and create a wonderful, JOYFUL life.

SEED 46
LOVE

It is said that at the end of your life when you face your creator, you will be evaluated not by what you did or how much you achieved but by how much you LOVED. This indicates that LOVE is the yardstick that measures your degree of spiritual development, and the level of evolvement you achieved in this lifetime. A highly evolved person knows that LOVE is the most powerful currency. The more you give LOVE, the more LOVE you will receive; this is one of the highest universal laws. LOVE is the surest way to enlightenment.

Where there is light, there is LOVE. LOVE is like a candle in the darkness that lights your way. LOVE is the healing balm that comforts the heart, soothes the soul, and frees the spirit to fly beyond unimaginable horizons. LOVE makes everything endurable. LOVE is the only real power and it can heal all suffering and transform any situation. LOVE has never ending patience; LOVE is always the answer.

When the heart is heavy or troubled, it is because you have forgotten and disconnected from LOVE. To be in the light is to be in LOVE, to always be aligned with LOVE brings great joy. Open yourself up to the light of LOVE, listen with your heart and let your heart speak. Open every chamber of the heart, even those parts that have been closed for a long time. Clear all barriers to LOVE and remember that you came here to experience LOVE, to give LOVE, to understand LOVE, and to fall in LOVE with life.

Reflections on
LOVE

LOVE is universal and it is not to be reserved just for a few people who are dear and close to you. LOVE is such a powerful, transformative force that it does not want to be restricted in any way. LOVE asks you to stay open and to allow it to flow freely through you. Let LOVE be free to inspire and elevate your every thought, word, and action.

Fill your heart with LOVE, let go of all neediness and just give and give until the waters of LOVE flow abundantly through you. Then you can become a channel of LOVE for the Divine Presence to work through you. There is no greater gift that you could ask for than being filled to the brim with the LOVE of the divine, and allowing your cup to run over.

LOVING yourself first is an essential part of learning to LOVE. When you decide to LOVE yourself enough, then you know that you are deserving of everything you desire. You will discover that there are no limits to LOVE, for pure LOVE is unconditional. This means there can be no feeling of lack, when your consciousness is filled with LOVE, then you will only choose and draw abundance to yourself. When you discover LOVE in yourself, you will also find LOVE in others and it will always be reflected back to you.

Look through the eyes of LOVE and your whole world will be transformed. You will see everything differently, as if you have been reborn. When you discover what it means to truly LOVE, then life becomes so beautiful, spontaneity blooms at every instant, and you tread a path that is filled with splendour and countless manifestations.

LOVE gives nothing but itself and asks nothing in return, it simply is. When you come to know LOVE, then you know who you are. Contemplate on LOVE, and meditate on LOVE. This is the greatest work you can do, both for yourself and for the world.

SEED 47

WISDOM

WISDOM sits at the seat of the soul; it holds its countenance with those who uphold the highest principles for humanity and does not suffer fools lightly. WISDOM is the territory of great sages and remarkable men and women. WISDOM does not seek to impress, neither to gain recognition, for it gains its credit through the richness that is inherent within WISDOM itself. WISDOM embraces the depths of learned knowledge and WISDOM is gained through the continual refinement of consciousness.

WISDOM enjoys the intelligence of a limitless mind that is open to all possibilities. WISDOM is aware that everything can be known, but what is needed is the spiritual evolvement that provides the access. WISDOM teaches us discernment and an acceptance of what is in the moment, knowing that the next moment may bring change and something totally different.

WISDOM makes no false promises, for it knows that your life's journey unfolds according to the intentions and understanding that you hold in your consciousness. As you are the creator of your reality, you reap the benefits of the Seeds that you sow. Therefore you must be WISE in your choices of which Seeds to sow. Sowing the Seeds of Transformation within your consciousness will open you to WISDOM.

Through deep WISDOM, cosmic knowledge becomes accessible. WISDOM can open the doors to the Akashic Records, the universal library wherein all known information throughout countless lifetimes is stored. The keys, the codes, and the initiations are all there; WISDOM provides the entry point.

Reflections on
WISDOM
——

WISDOM comes from beyond space and time and it arises out of the depths of being and is nurtured by the stillness and silence that is found in deep meditation. WISDOM needs time to bloom. The ancient ones and great sages understood this well and therefore taught patience and perseverance as steps towards developing WISDOM.

WISDOM is the flowering from within, the ripening that occurs when the time is right. WISDOM knows what is right in the moment, but it never judges, it just observes and respects and acknowledges that the right consequences will follow the right actions. WISDOM understands the laws of karma and knows how they work and therefore counsels you to be meticulous in every thought, word, and action. WISDOM guides you when to speak and when not to speak, what to say and what not to say, and to listen carefully to what any particular situation requires in order to express the highest WISDOM.

WISDOM transcends the mind: it is beyond thought, it does not get caught up in the world of dramas but neither does it suppress nor ignore. WISDOM embraces the most expansive viewpoint, the clarity of which does not need to take sides. WISDOM is able to remain detached yet at the same time loving, and compassionate.

WISDOM wants to be expressed, to make the unmanifest manifest. How you live your life is your choice, but let it be guided by the hand of WISDOM and by the WISE one within that sees and knows.

SEED 48
WHOLENESS

———

From the wisdom of the Divine Presence and the transcendental, pure flame of awareness comes the vision of being WHOLE: a vision of living in a world that is filled with love and compassion and deep concern for our fellow human beings. Those who work with integrity and have the ability to envision a world that is WHOLE and without pain or suffering, can help bring it about. There is a lot of work to be done and the journey begins with each individual healing back into WHOLENESS.

WHOLENESS is a state of perfection that creates a synthesis that brings everything together and leaves nothing out. Inherent within WHOLENESS is the ability to see things differently from a higher perspective and to become a co-creator of the process. The wish to become WHOLE again, to find and synthesize all aspects of the self begins when you are aware that this is what you truly desire. Then the strive towards attaining WHOLENESS becomes a priority and nothing can stand in your way.

WHOLENESS requires healing on all levels: the physical, emotional, mental, and spiritual, and the integration of all four. WHOLENESS also includes healing the separation from the Divine and realizing that when you work with the powerful trinity of light, love, and wisdom, then anything can be healed.

Creating WHOLENESS takes time; it is an ongoing process of healing and growth. With time you get clearer on what else needs to happen, to move you closer towards WHOLENESS. The more you come from a place of love and are attentive and watchful, the more you allow yourself to release whatever is still in the way of the unfoldment of your true perfection. Then the flowering and the blossoming of your true essence becomes evident. The closer you are to your essential nature, your ultimate beingness, the more harmonious and WHOLE you will become.

Reflections on
WHOLENESS

The more you embrace WHOLENESS, the deeper the level of healing that occurs as you become more conscious of what still needs healing. WHOLENESS becomes a way of being with yourself that is non-judgemental and instead is about learning how to support and nourish yourself in the process of becoming WHOLE again. Then your life becomes a remarkable journey, the reflection of which can change everything around you.

WHOLENESS attracts because it is so very potent. Once you recognize that you live in a limitless world with infinite possibilities, then WHOLENESS will help you to perceive new and expanded realities, which will draw to you whatever you desire. Everyone is travelling the journey, but to do so consciously moves you more quickly towards WHOLENESS and teaches you not to be afraid to release the barriers or resistance that you may still be holding.

The closer you come to WHOLENESS, the easier it becomes to make more conscious choices that positively assist your journey of unfoldment. Then the process of creating and manifesting becomes a wonderful, creative, expression of WHOLENESS.

WHOLENESS encompasses everything and develops our admiration for the perfection of the universe and for the remarkable and unexpected ways that things come together and fall into place.

UNITY

———

From a place of wholeness, you naturally move towards UNITY consciousness. You want to share what you have learnt and gained for yourself. You no longer think only in terms of yourself but for the greater whole, and you desire for healing to occur on a much broader scale. UNITY calls for global healing, for the healing of separation and division and the reuniting of the global family. UNITY seeks an acceptance of all races, cultures, and religions; acknowledging that on a deeper level we are all one and that each human being needs to recognize every other human being and that this is of the utmost importance. UNITY is inclusive and focuses on the healing of the world and the transformation of the world consciousness, and the current state of affairs.

UNITY appreciates the sacredness of all life and the inter-connectedness of all things and it seeks to UNITE rather than divide and always remains open with compassion. UNITY accepts and respects both the UNITY and the diversity of the global family, and recognizes that everyone has a unique contribution to make to the whole. This can only be achieved when the barriers and prejudices between people and nations are dissolved.

Everything and everyone is intricately connected through a universal web, which is made up of experiences, visions, cosmic threads, energetic configurations, and a dynamic pulsating life force that beats in every heart and soul. This is the UNIFIED field of consciousness: an unlimited, expansive, creative field of all possibilities.

A person's state of consciousness, and level of spiritual development determine how much conscious access there is to the UNIFIED field. Having the desire to attain UNITY consciousness ascertains that one is already on the path and that the inner longing for a deeper connection and communion with every aspect of life will be fulfilled.

Reflections on
UNITY

—

When the awareness of the interconnectedness and interdependence of all things begins to stir within the consciousness of the individual, then the wish to know more about how to participate as an active spiritual seeker grows stronger. The need to be of service and to make a difference in the world becomes an important focal point of the person's life. The focus is no longer on ego based individual satisfaction but a desire to selflessly become more involved in playing an active part in the creation and weaving of the tapestry of life in a way that will benefit the whole of humanity.

When UNITY motivates your every thought and action, then your life is filled with a passionate purpose, and you know you have a destiny to fulfil and you allow spirit to guide you step by step. UNITY inspires the need for communication, sharing, cooperation, collaboration, and purposeful living.

When one dissolves into the consciousness of the all that is, the oneness and UNITY of all life, then your whole being is saturated in bliss and the expression of this blissful state is uplifting, inspiring, and transforming to all those around you.

Think about how it would be to take every step of your life with an unlimited connection through UNIFICATION with everyone and everything. You would never experience another moment of isolation because you know that in every moment you are always connected and actively participating in the co-creation of this beautiful web of life.

SEED 50

MIRACLES

———

MIRACLES come from the domain of the celestial; they are gifts from the transcendent, which are beyond the known physical laws. MIRACLES appear unexpectedly by interrupting and changing karmic patterns. MIRACLES create sudden shifts that reorganize events; they transcend space and time and reflect the unlimited laws of eternity. MIRACLES can release the past, empower the present, and thereby change the expected future.

MIRACLES have an immeasurable sphere of influence; they are beyond normal perception and are ordained from the angelic realms. When you believe in MIRACLES you work on a level of existence that aligns your experiences with the divine creation, and you co-create together. At this level there is no room for doubt or fear, these have long been cast aside and replaced by spiritual vision and spiritual empowerment and a growing sense of unity consciousness that thinks in terms of the greater whole.

MIRACLES are universal blessings that are showered upon us every day, but they are often not recognized or appreciated for what they are. Open your mind to MIRACLE minded consciousness and embrace a new reality that you may never have even dreamt of; it is there, waiting to be experienced.

Reflections on
MIRACLES

MIRACLES are everywhere. Life itself is a MIRACLE, as are the processes of conception, birth, and our whole existence. When you develop MIRACLE minded consciousness and come to understand the process, you see that nothing is at random or by chance. You will also understand the subtleties of the process and that by shifting your consciousness, even one degree, will bring about changes. The results of these changes can be outstanding and are called MIRACLES. This is consciousness at work and at play within itself, creating and producing MIRACULOUS results.

The master alchemists understood the alchemical process of how one state or situation could be transformed into another. Their craft was in creating MIRACLES. You too can become a master alchemist of your life when you learn how to work with the laws of nature and creation and can then create MIRACLES in your life.

MIRACLES occur within sacred space; they require an absolute purity of mind, a heart that is filled with love, and detachment to the outcome. MIRACLES come from the source and they are an expression of pure love and they are a natural part of life. Don't think of MIRACLES only in terms of healing, but also in ways to shift and change situations that bring you the help and support you need. MIRACLES create openings so that the unexpected can come into your life.

MIRACLES are a medium of communication; they renew, create, and recreate, and when they touch your life, they bring profound and lasting change. Use your mind creatively and develop MIRACLE minded consciousness, then the whole universe will become an accessible resource that offers you all possible assistance and abundance. Unconditional love, an abundance of light energy, wholeness, and unity can create MIRACLES out of ordinary things.

MIRACLE minded consciousness is the alignment to the domain of love and enlightenment, which is infinite and timeless.

SEED 51
ENLIGHTENMENT

ENLIGHTENMENT is the evolutionary process of becoming, of growing into the fullness of your being. ENLIGHTENMENT is the awakening and transformation of consciousness that leads you to a light filled, loving, and blissful state of existence. This beautiful state is often described as going home. ENLIGHTENMENT means you have reached the vastness of existential knowingness, which is beyond even the furthest of horizons. For most people, ENLIGHTENMENT means taking the long journey through countless lifetimes until eventually there is a breakthrough as you finally pass through the clouds that have veiled your vision and the barriers of illusion. Then you move into an illumined, loving existence that sustains your whole being.

ENLIGHTENMENT is the beginning of the long journey home, returning to that which you knew and have forgotten and at last remember. It is all there, encoded within your cosmic memory in the cells of your body, but you need the right keys to unlock the codes. ENLIGHTENMENT reveals that there is nowhere to go, for home is within you and you carry your home with you wherever you go.

ENLIGHTENMENT offers a whole new way of seeing; where everything is revealed to you. As your cosmic vision develops, it gives you access to unlimited, expansive views of what is possible. Through the universal alignment, which ENLIGHTENMENT brings, your spiritual vision increases day by day, enabling you to tune into the collective consciousness of thought and to reflect on how to become a conscious, active server in transforming the world.

We stand on the brink of the dawning of a new age, known as the Golden Age. As we move further into this new age, many changes will occur on earth. Those that are fully awake are watching this unfoldment with great interest. As globally people awaken to the power of who they really are and move into their ENLIGHTENMENT process, they will be able to serve humanity as lightworkers and peacemakers who will hold the balance during this important time of transition.

Reflections on
ENLIGHTENMENT

———

As you awaken to the ENLIGHTENMENT process, you will feel spiritually so alive. You will feel it in every cell of your body as every cell is filled with radiant light. You will breathe the breath of life and appreciate the prana, the life force energy that sustains life, and feel it pulsating vibrantly through you.

An ENLIGHTENED person cannot be held back, their energy is always moving, pulsating, giving, sharing, and lovingly being of service. In return the universe brings all the support that is needed and ensures that everything is well taken care of. The potential is there within you, the passion and dynamism to create and manifest and make a difference in the world through your own unique contribution. Every Seed planted will come to its full fruition and help the evolvement of your ENLIGHTENMENT process. Keep working with all the Seeds until you attain ENLIGHTENMENT and then the essential light within you will come forward and ENLIGHTEN every thought, feeling, and expression that you have. There are no shortcuts; you have to do the work, to take the journey. All the necessary assistance will be given if you respond openly and honestly from the highest level of integrity. Become a conscious creator attuned to the cosmic forces and then life will be an adventurous journey towards ENLIGHTENMENT.

The magic is in the present moment. If you stand still enough and be patient, you will discover there is only bliss; this is the revelation of ENLIGHTENMENT. Surrender to a greater power, to the Divine Presence, and join the ENLIGHTENED ones who bring peace and healing to the world.

Continue your awakening into ENLIGHTENMENT by spending time within the stillness and silence of the sacred sanctuary of meditation. From there all blessings will be bestowed and ENLIGHTENMENT will be revealed.

SEED 52
I AM

Who AM I? This is the question that philosophers and spiritual seekers have asked for eons. Yet the answer is simple, it lies in the question, I AM. The recognition of I AM in its ultimate existence and profound understanding brings incredible release and the cessation of the need to search further. It is so simple that most often the mind struggles to comprehend because it likes to complicate things and does not trust simplicity.

When the first glimpses of enlightenment begin to come, then the I AM is revealed and nothing can veil your consciousness; the way is made clear. The I AM is the way, it is the tool, the technique, and the sacred mantra of the ascended masters that is given to those who are ready to step out of illusion and move into the radiance and illumination of the Divine Presence.

The sacredness, the purity, and the grace that is required to align with the Divine Presence embodies every Seed that has been given until now. You have been given a whole year of Seeds to work with, and these will enlighten and transform your consciousness as you continue to work with them again and again. When these Seeds have been well mastered, then the I AM presence will step forth and become the central core around which everything else revolves.

The I AM is a spark of the divine; it is a thread that connects you to the source of all creation. It is a reflection of the all that is, of what has been, what is, and of everything that can ever be. Therefore when you choose to work with the I AM and to embody it, live it, and breathe it, your whole being will expand and move way beyond what you have known until now and this can change your whole existence.

When you are anchored in the Divine Presence, the I AM, you are anchored in truth and spiritual power, which is as solid as a rock. Nothing else can give you the security and a sense of being held and looked after as the I AM presence.

The I AM presence is fully awakened consciousness, awake and illumined within itself. It is the sacred all embracing power of all life everywhere.

Reflections on
I AM
———

Continue to work with the following affirmations or mantras to open your consciousness to the spiritually illuminating power of the Divine Presence.

I AM

I AM that I AM

I AM nothing, I AM everything, I AM

I AM Divine Presence

I AM beyond space and time

I AM light

I AM love

I AM wisdom

I AM spiritually empowered

I AM radiant

I AM bliss

I AM the Christ energy within and without

I AM all that is

I AM that I AM

I AM

The I AM presence is the sacred mantra that aligns you with the beauty, the mystery, and the sacredness of all life. May your journey be truly blessed.

LIVING WITH VISION

The Seeds are incredibly powerful tools of transformation and each one will continue to open many doors. Keep using the Seeds in your life and reread them over and over again and watch how your consciousness expands moment by moment, day by day. Remember the Seeds are a gift from the Gods and the Goddesses, share them wherever you go, invite others to work with them too, and help scatter the Seeds all over the world.

Based upon the teachings of the Seeds, I have created my Living with Vision webpage, to help you explore further how to manifest the vision that you desire. I invite you to visit my webpage http://www.livingwithvision.com and to subscribe to my monthly newsletter.

Love, light, and blessings
Maggie Erotokritou
visionquest@spidernet.com.cy

A Tribute to Lightworkers
Around the World

———

By Maggie Erotokritou

As I go into the silence
to connect with my being,
I settle down into the oneness
that pervades my soul.
In this moment I know that I AM.
I breathe, I feel, I sense, I allow.

It is a rare moment of unity,
which once tasted cannot be forgotten.
It is the remembrance of the Christlight
that surrounds and permeates everything.

I feel the light pouring through me,
down through the crown chakra
into every cell of my body.
It fills my mind with wisdom and clarity,
and opens my heart to love and compassion.
I am open, I am receptive,
and my boundaries and limitations are released.

The light energy pulsates
like the hum of the universe.
It is perfection, blissful and unifying.
My soul recognizes this pulsation
and longs to hold onto this treasured moment,
but knows it to be fleeting in order
to make way for the next experience.

The light envelopes me like a cloak of wonder,
embracing the totality of who I AM,
and who I may become.

I feel the light reaching out from me to you
and coming back from you to me.
Outward and onward, sharing and connecting,
creating the most beautiful network of light.
May we share in the beauty, carrying our
torches of light out into the world.

And in doing so, let us remember
to always give thanks again and again.
For to have the opportunity to be of service
to mankind, is to share in a great honour
and to be truly blessed.
May love and light prevail on earth!

GLOSSARY

HUNDREDTH MONKEY EFFECT – when one person in one part of the world starts doing something, and on an unconscious level another person in another part of the world, or in the local community, picks it up telepathically and starts doing the same thing without any verbal communication. Then suddenly more and more people start doing the same thing, and it spreads and creates what is known as the hundredth monkey effect.

BODYTALK – a unique, holistic, healing approach of energy medicine, which allows the body and mind to come back to balance and heal itself right down to the cellular level. Check out the BodyTalk section on my webpage. http://www.livingwithvision.com

SHAKTI – the feminine power of the Goddess or Divine Feminine energy.

CRYSTALLINE CHRIST ENERGY – the purest light energy that comes from the source of all creation

VAASTU – an ancient Indian science that helps create harmony and balance within the environment. The principles are based upon becoming one with nature, and bringing everything into the right alignment so as to be able to live in a harmonious way.

VIOLET FLAME – spiritual alchemists use the violet flame, the violet-coloured energy, to transmute and heal the mind, body, and soul and for the higher work of self transformation.

BIBLIOGRAPHY
———

Spiritual books that helped along the path:

Barks, Coleman and Green, Michael. *The Illumined Rumi*. New York: Broadway Books, 1997.

Cousins, David. *A Handbook for Lightworkers*. Bath: Barton House, 1993.

Foundation for Inner Peace. *A Course in Miracles*. New York: Penguin Books, 1975.

Goldsmith, Joel S. *Living the Illumined Life*. Atlanta: Acropolis Books, 1971.

Hanh, Thich Nhat. *The Miracle of Mindfulness*. London: Rider, 1975.

Mascaro, Juan. *The Dhammapada*. London: Penguin Books, 1973

Morya, El. *The Chela and the Path: Keys to Soul Mastery in the Aquarian Age*. Corwin Springs: Summit University Press, 1975.

Mother Meera. *Answers*. New York: Meeramma Publications, 1991.

Sri Swami Satchidananda. *The Yoga Sutras of Patanjali*. Yogaville, Virginia: Integral Yoga Publications, 1978.

Swami Sivananda. *Sadhana*. Himalayas: The Divine Life Society, 1998.

Yogananda, Paramahansa. *Autobiography of a Yogi*. Los Angeles: Self-Realization Fellowship, 1946.

Yogananda, Paramahansa. *Journey to Self-Realization*. Los Angeles: Self-Realization Fellowship, 1997.

A Little Light on Angels
by
DIANA COOPER

"I believe in angels" is the title of a well-known
song — but do we really?
With this book,we meet everyday folks who have
experienced angels in their lives.Yes, angels do exist: they
are highly evolved beings that have a lighter and faster
vibration than humans, and are normally invisible to us.
However, many of them have chosen to serve mankind and
are available to help, support, heal, and guide us — all we
have to do is ask! There are small angels who care for the
little daily tasks and enormous beings that overlight great
universal projects. There are angels who can assist in healing
and other who attend celebrations and rituals.
A Little Light on Angels gives us guidance on how we can
call on themfor help and companionship in our lives.
We are surrounded by angels, all we have to do is raise our
consciousness to become aware of them and communicate
with them, to welcome them into our lives and allow the
joy, light, and peace of their presence into our hearts.

"This whole matter of dealing with Angels is far more
business-like than the uninitiated might think, and it is
not just about peace, healing, and a healthy aura.
Angels can also be called upon to solve practical problems,
and there is even an Angel of parking spaces!"
RONALD WHITE, THE SUNDAY TIMES

128 pages paperback – ISBN 1-899171-51-7

A New Light on Ascension
by
DIANA COOPER

It has been ten years since Kumeka, Master of the Eighth
Ray, introduced himself to Diana Cooper and began to
meld his consciousness with hers.

A Little Light on Ascension presented the information he
impressed on Diana at the time, but since then, much has
changed on our planet, and Kumeka has recently imparted
further information. This knowledge, previously offered to
just a few, is now available to millions of lightworkers eager
to assist in the task of moving this planet into the light.
Yes, ascending into the higher realms can be achieved in
this lifetime. We may have to work at it, but all the tools
and information we need are now available to us thanks to
A New Light on Ascension. However, be prepared, this
journey is not for the fainthearted! Kumeka does not offer
a quick fix; he invites and encourages each one of us to join
the millions on the planet now actively working towards a
joyful life of spirit.

"Diana Cooper's *A Little Light on Ascension* is the book that
reminds me why I am here and what it is all about.
To say I find it an inspiration is an understatement;
to describe is as my bible would not be an exaggeration."
SUSAN CLARK, THE SUNDAY TIMES

208 pages paperback – ISBN 1-89409-035-3

Angels of Light Cards
by
DIANA COOPER

Angels are waiting and happy to help you at all times. Under
Spiritual Law they cannot step in until you ask. Whenever you have
a problem, there is an angel standing by you, awaiting your
permission to assist.

Angels cannot and will not help you if you ask for something from
neediness and greed. Nor will they help you receive something
which is not spiritually right. Recognise your authority and make
your requests from wisdom and strength. You may also ask the
angels to help someone else for his or her highest good, not
necessarily for what you think that highest good might be. Your
thoughts to that person create a rainbow bridge along which the
angels can travel to help him or her. You can also ask the
angels to help the planet.

Each of the 52 Angel Cards included in this deck represent a
different Angel quality, and can be used for guidance, inspiration,
and affirmation. The cards will help you tune in to the higher
vibrations of the Angels, and allow you to feel the helping hands of
these beings at all times. Following the inspiration of the Angels will
raise your consciousness,which will automatically help you attract
to yourself people and situations of a higher vibratory level and
release old negative thought patterns. Carry these cards with you
wherever you go and use them to remind yourself of the presence,
guidance, and help of the Angels in your life, always and everywhere.
You are never alone or lost when the Angels are with you.

Pack of 52 cards + booklet + velvet bag – ISBN 1-899171-14-2

FINDHORN PRESS

Books, Card Sets,
CDs & DVDs
that inspire and uplift

For a complete catalogue,
please contact:

Findhorn Press Ltd
305a The Park, Findhorn
Forres IV36 3TE
Scotland, UK

Telephone +44-(0)1309-690582
Fax +44-(0)1309-690036
eMail info@findhornpress.com

or consult our catalogue online
(with secure order facility) on
www.findhornpress.com